NEW DIRECTIONS FOR TEACHING AND LEARNING

Robert J. Menges, *Northwestern University*
EDITOR-IN-CHIEF

Marilla D. Svinicki, *University of Texas, Austin*
ASSOCIATE EDITOR

Teaching in the Information Age: The Role of Educational Technology

Michael J. Albright
University of Hawaii at Manoa

David L. Graf
Iowa State University

EDITORS

Number 51, Fall 1992

JOSSEY-BASS PUBLISHERS
San Francisco

TEACHING IN THE INFORMATION AGE: THE ROLE OF
EDUCATIONAL TECHNOLOGY
Michael J. Albright, David L. Graf (eds.)
New Directions for Teaching and Learning, no. 51
Robert J. Menges, Editor-in-Chief
Marilla D. Svinicki, Associate Editor

Microfilm copies of issues and articles are available in 16mm and 35mm,
as well as microfiche in 105mm, through University Microfilms Inc., 300
North Zeeb Road, Ann Arbor, Michigan 48106.

LC 85-644763   ISSN 0271-0633   ISBN 1-55542-744-8

NEW DIRECTIONS FOR TEACHING AND LEARNING is part of The Jossey-Bass
Higher and Adult Education Series and is published quarterly by Jossey-
Bass Inc., Publishers, 350 Sansome Street, San Francisco, California 94104.
Second-class postage paid at San Francisco, California, and at additional
mailing offices. POSTMASTER: Send address changes to Jossey-Bass Inc.,
Publishers, 350 Sansome Street, San Francisco, California 94104.

SUBSCRIPTIONS for 1992 cost $45.00 for individuals and $60.00 for institutions, agencies, and libraries.

EDITORIAL CORRESPONDENCE should be sent to Robert J. Menges, Northwestern University, Center for the Teaching Professions, 2003 Sheridan
Road, Evanston, Illinois 60208-2610.

Cover photograph by Richard Blair/Color & Light © 1990.

The paper used in this journal is acid-free and meets the strictest
guidelines in the United States for recycled paper (50 percent
recycled waste, including 10 percent post-consumer waste). Manu-
factured in the United States of America.

CONTENTS

EDITORS' NOTES   1
Michael J. Albright, David L. Graf

1. Instructional Technology and the Faculty Member   7
Michael J. Albright, David L. Graf
Instructional technology is presented as a broad concept embracing teaching methods, classrooms, and the training of faculty members, in addition
to the traditional concerns for equipment and materials.

2. New Directions in Presentation Graphics: 17
Impact on Teaching and Learning
J. Thomas Head
Current trends in the development and utilization of computer-generated
presentation graphics are reviewed.

3. Multimedia and the Teaching-Learning Process in   33
Higher Education
Annette C. Lamb
The marriage of computers, audio and video playback systems, and optical
storage devices presents faculty with unique, effective, and exciting instruc-
tional tools for the future.

4. Academic Computing: How to Address the Teaching and   43
Learning Challenge
Margret Hazen
The enormous potential of computing in support of instruction is tempered
by rapid technological change, funding limitations, and organizational
issues.

5. Computer Communications and Learning   55
Beryl L. Bellman
The roles and advantages of computer conferencing as a delivery system
for college instruction are discussed, with examples drawn from the
BESTNET project.

6. Distance Education: Meeting Diverse Learners' Needs in a   65
Changing World
Marcia A. Baird, Mavis K. Monson
The opportunities and challenges presented by distance education are
discussed, as higher education looks for ways to better serve off-campus
learners.

7. The Emerging Potential of Virtual Reality in   77
Postsecondary Education
James P. Randall
Virtual reality is described as an emerging technology with revolutionary
possibilities for providing hands-on active learning environments that sim-
ulate the real world.

8. The Research Library and Emerging Information Technology   83
Lucy Siefert Wegner
The dramatic influence of information technology on academic libraries is
raising new questions about the basic concept of a library and the future
roles of librarians and patrons.

9. The Future of Campus Media Centers   91
Michael J. Albright
Campus media centers play an essential role in supporting college teaching
but are often handicapped by the lack of recognition, inappropriate reporting structures, and absence of strong leadership.

10. Faculty Development's Role in Improving   101
Undergraduate Education
David L. Graf, Michael J. Albright, Daniel W. Wheeler
The importance of and current trends in services known as faculty, instruc-
tional, organizational, and personal development are described.

INDEX   111

EDITORS' NOTES

> The history of modern education is littered with the trash of technology left behind by unrealistic purchases, naive users, and vendor representatives working on a quota system.
> —Polley, 1977

Instructional technology has always seemed to have extraordinary potential for transforming higher education. Ashby (1967) felt that the emergence and use of electronic technologies was the fourth revolution in education, following the establishment of public schools, the adoption of the written word as a tool of education, and the widespread distribution and use of textbooks. The Carnegie Commission on Higher Education (1972, p. 1) reported that "new technology may provide the greatest single opportunity for academic change on and off campus," and that by the year 2000 "a significant proportion of instruction in higher education on campus may be carried on through information technology—perhaps in a range of 10 to 20 percent."

It is now clear that the Carnegie Commission's predictions were unrealistic. Most of its recommendations were ignored and forgotten. As the opening quote from Polley (1977) indicates, many institutions invested in technology-based instructional systems that were misused or unused and eventually found their way into storerooms, leaving behind bitterness toward technology among the faculty members and administrators responsible for its purchase. In reality, all too often the fault lay not with the technology but with those who failed to plan carefully for its use and provide the supporting infrastructure and ongoing funding base necessary to ensure its success. Nonetheless, instructional technology developed a questionable reputation among many faculty members. In his highly influential book on faculty development, Gaff (1975, p. 73) observed that "disdain for technological 'aids' runs deep in faculty culture."

There is little question that instructional technology has had minimal impact on college teaching. According to Donald McNeil (1988), former president of the University of Mid-America and later a senior program officer for the Agency for Educational Development, the vast majority of faculty members still are either apathetic about or openly resist the use of computers and videotapes as instructional tools. Classroom technologies rarely achieve prominent mention in academic development plans. Support services such as media centers are often treated as peripheral to the institution's mission, with librarians or paraprofessionals placed in charge.

Moreover, instructional technology does not appear to be part of the vision of those who influence change in postsecondary education. In a recent open letter to higher education leadership, Stephen W. Gilbert (1990), vice president of EDUCOM, complained that information technology seemed to be overlooked during discussions of the future of postsecondary education and the improvement of college teaching. He emphasized that he did not feel that technology was being rejected, just never considered.

Nonetheless, the frenetic pace of technological change in society at large is carrying over to our campuses. Exciting new instructional programs and services involving technology are being established all across the country, some of which have significant implications for the way that teaching and learning will be conducted in the future. Consider these examples: (1) Indiana University-Purdue University at Indianapolis has established the goal of becoming the national prototype for electronic campuses (Elmore, 1991a). Concurrently, the newest campus of the California State University System, in San Marcos, is being constructed as a "model educational community of the 21st century," featuring an Advanced Telecommunications Platform to facilitate instructional communications across campus and around the world ("University of the Future . . . ," 1991, p. 6). (2) Many colleges and universities are installing state-of-the-art multimedia projection systems and faculty workstations in classrooms. Descriptions have been published or presented for facilities at the University of North Carolina at Chapel Hill (Conway, 1990), Vanderbilt University (Watkins, 1991c), Brigham Young University (Fawson and VanUitert, 1990), Indiana University-Purdue University at Indianapolis (Elmore, 1991b), Kent State University (Kerstetter and Minno, 1992), State University of New York at Buffalo (Anderson and Cichocki, 1992), and University of California at Santa Cruz (Dickens and Duggan, 1992). (3) The National Technological University delivers seven hundred graduate engineering courses to twelve hundred students nationwide, exclusively by satellite, and is expected to be one of the top ten universities in the country awarding M.S. degrees in engineering by 1995 (Marek, 1991). (4) The Texas A&M University System recently inaugurated an interactive, high-speed data and compressed video network that links three campus locations with eleven other university sites around the state. The system permits interactive video, audio, and data transmission, for instructional or videoconferencing purposes, among as many as fourteen different groups simultaneously ("New Video Network . . . ," 1991). (5) McGraw-Hill and the campus bookstore at the University of California at San Diego (UCSD) are collaborating on a project that allows UCSD faculty members to custom-design their textbooks, using a new electronic publishing center, to meet specific classroom needs (Watkins, 1991a). (6) The *Chronicle of Higher Education* is now available on an experimental basis to faculty and students at the University of Southern California through the campuswide computer network (Watkins, 1991b).

This volume, *Teaching in the Information Age,* examines some of the current trends in instructional technology and discusses their implications for teaching and learning in the postsecondary setting. The term *instructional technology* is used here with the broadest possible reference to include not only the software and hardware *products* commonly associated with instructional technology but the basic *processes* of teaching and learning as well. We believe that there is a "technology of instruction" that incorporates everything educators know about how people learn and the strategies and resources used to teach them. All of the instructional systems and support services featured in this volume represent various forms of this technology. We have placed a special emphasis on specific applications in the teaching-learning setting.

In Chapter One, Michael J. Albright and David L. Graf provide a detailed discussion of what instructional technology is and how it fits within the context of college teaching. They argue that instructional technology products should be regarded not as panaceas or frills but as tools that can be manipulated by faculty members to stimulate learning. The chapter concludes with an analysis of the resistance to instructional technology and offers suggestions for overcoming this resistance.

Chapters Two through Seven are devoted to specific instructional delivery systems. J. Thomas Head, in Chapter Two, describes state-of-the-art presentation graphics, manifested most commonly in overhead transparencies, photographic slides, and hard copies. He explains the benefits of visualizing course information and discusses the systems currently used by both individual faculty members and graphics professionals to produce effective, aesthetically pleasing materials.

Although *multimedia* once referred to simple slide-tape presentations, the term now applies to a computer-based system incorporating video, audio, and digital storage media. Annette C. Lamb, in Chapter Three, describes common multimedia systems and explains how nonlinear access to information can provide an active, productive learning environment. Her chapter concludes with a discussion of barriers to the integration of multimedia into higher education and an assessment of the future of multimedia.

An estimated 5.7 million personal computers had been installed on America's college and university campuses by the end of 1991 (Schwebach, 1991). The dramatic evolution of academic computing in higher education is recounted by Margret Hazen in Chapter Four. Hazen discusses the impact of computers on the teaching and learning process and then offers strategies for the effective placement and operation of academic computing support units.

As the number of personal computers has grown, interest in using them to deliver courses has increased. Entire graduate degree programs are now available online from at least eight universities, with most or all coursework conducted via computer communications networks (Earnest, 1992). In Chapter Five, Beryl L. Bellman describes the Binational English and Spanish Tele-communications Network (BESTNET), which now provides three types of computer-based courses in the United States, Canada, and Latin America and soon will be expanded to Africa. The effectiveness of BESTNET with women, minorities, and people with disabilities is of particular interest.

Distance education is a phenomenon approaching boom proportions on a worldwide basis. Marcia A. Baird and Mavis K. Monson explain why in Chapter Six. They describe the characteristics that differentiate between successful and unsuccessful distance education systems. They discuss current trends and then conclude their chapter with a detailed analysis of the implications of distance education for higher education institutions.

In Chapter Seven, James P. Randall explores the potential of virtual reality, a technology that is beginning to have applications in industry and the military but remains at the experimental stage in higher education. Randall describes virtual reality technology and details several current research-and-development projects.

Chapters Eight through Ten focus on current trends in instructional support services for college and university faculty. Lucy Siefert Wegner, in Chapter Eight, discusses the dramatic implications of information technology for research libraries. She describes the technologies that are providing alternatives to print and speculates how library patrons will conduct literature searches in the future. She concludes by asking questions about the future of books, the role of the librarian, and the library as a whole.

The evolution of instructional technology has had a profound effect on the role of the campus media center. In Chapter Nine, Michael J. Albright portrays the emerging mission of media centers and emphasizes the importance of their services to campus instructional programs. He describes how their ability to support and strengthen academic programs has been seriously hampered by lack of recognition, inappropriate reporting structures, and the absence of strong leadership.

The improvement of teaching skills among faculty members is widely viewed as a form of instructional development and is therefore an instructional technology function. In Chapter Ten, David L. Graf, Michael J. Albright, and Daniel W. Wheeler differentiate among faculty development, instructional development, organizational development, and personal development and then describe the forms in which these services appear in higher education today. They provide guidance for the staffing of faculty development programs and conclude with an assessment of the future of these efforts.

Michael J. Albright
David L. Graf
Editors

References

Anderson, J. A., and Cichocki, R. R. "Media Equipped Classrooms: Giving Attention to the Teaching Station." Paper presented at the annual convention of the Association for Educational Communications and Technology, Washington, D.C., February 1992.

Ashby, E. "Machines, Understanding, and Learning: Reflections on Technology in Education." *Graduate Journal*, 1967, 7 (2), 359–372.

Carnegie Commission on Higher Education. *The Fourth Revolution: Instructional Technology in Higher Education.* New York: McGraw-Hill, 1972.

Conway, K. L. *Master Classrooms: Classroom Design with Technology in Mind.* Institute for Academic Technology, University of North Carolina at Chapel Hill Technology in Higher Education Series, no. 3. McKinney, Tex.: Academic Computing, 1990.

Dickens, J. L., and Duggan, B. "Successful Facilities for Media Presentations." Paper presented at the annual convention of the Association for Educational Communications and Technology, Washington, D.C., February 1992.

Earnest, C. "Happily Modeming to School." *Online Access*, 1992, 7 (1), 6–8.

Elmore, G. C. *Learning Technologies Annual Report.* Indianapolis: Learning Technologies, Indiana University-Purdue University, 1991a.

Elmore, G. C. "Planning and Developing a Multimedia Learning Environment." *T.H.E. Journal*, 1991b, 18 (7), 83–88.

Fawson, E. C., and VanUitert, D. D. "The Technology Classroom: Alternatives for Future Planning." *TechTrends*, 1990, 35 (4), 28–34.

Gaff, J. G. *Toward Faculty Renewal: Advances in Faculty, Instructional, and Organizational Development.* San Francisco: Jossey-Bass, 1975.

Gilbert, S. W. "Tomorrow's Faculty and Information Technology: An Opportunity Lost?" *EUIT Newsletter*, 1990, 4 (2), 6.

Kerstetter, J. P., and Minno, R. A. "Designing Facilities for Large-Screen Data and Video Projection Systems." Paper presented at the annual convention of the Association for Educational Communications and Technology, Washington, D.C., February 1992.

McNeil, D. R. "Status of Technology in Higher Education: A Reassessment." Paper presented at the 2nd annual conference on Interactive Technology and Telecommunications, Augusta, Maine, September 1988.

Marek, S. "Distance Education: Transforming Traditional Learning." *Satellite Communications*, 1991, 15 (7), 18–22.

"New Video Network at Texas A&M University System." *Educational Technology*, 1991, 31 (8), 8.

Polley, E. "The Effects of ATS-6." Paper presented at the National Institute of Education conference on Educational Applications of Satellites, Washington, D.C., February 1977.

Schwebach, L. "PCs and Education: Part 2." *PC Today*, 1991, 5 (10), 33–37.

"University of the Future Planned for California." *Educational Technology*, 1991, 31 (12), 6.

Watkins, B. T. "San Diego Campus and McGraw-Hill Create Custom Texts." *Chronicle of Higher Education*, Nov. 6, 1991a, p. A25.

Watkins, B. T. "USC Puts Text of 'The Chronicle' on Its Campus Network." *Chronicle of Higher Education*, Oct. 9, 1991b, p. A26.

Watkins, B. T. "Vanderbilt's Chancellor: A Tireless Advocate for Computer Technology." *Chronicle of Higher Education*, Sept. 4, 1991c, p. A28.

MICHAEL J. ALBRIGHT is director of the Center for Instructional Support, University of Hawaii at Manoa, Honolulu.

DAVID L. GRAF is coordinator for instructional development at the Media Resources Center, Iowa State University, Ames.

Instructional technology is a broad concept that embraces virtually every aspect of teaching and learning. As we approach the twenty-first century, societal pressures will force faculty members to overcome their longstanding resistance to the instructional use of technology.

Instructional Technology and the Faculty Member

Michael J. Albright, David L. Graf

This is the first volume of New Directions for Teaching and Learning in ten years to be totally dedicated to the topic of instructional technology. In the last series volume on this topic, Christopher Knapper (1982a, p. 1) lamented that despite the technological advances that so strongly influence our lives, "A good many contemporary university students probably find themselves taught by methods largely unchanged from those experienced by their parents or grandparents." We can make essentially the same claim today. The microcomputer has helped many faculty members to become more comfortable in using technology, but instructional use remains minimal.

Why has technology not had a greater impact on college teaching? The reasons have been variously identified as conservative institutional structures that inhibit change, faculty commitment to traditional teaching methods, a reward system that does not recognize efforts to improve teaching, and overt fear of technology (McNeil, 1988); the lack of recognition of technology by administrators and faculty as an integral part of the curriculum and under-graduate experience (Green, 1991); insufficient financial resources that enable colleges and universities to invest in technology, the rapid pace of technological change, the complexity of some technology-based instructional systems, disproportionate access to technology from one academic unit to another, the shortage of high-quality software, the time required for faculty to learn to use technology and develop needed materials, the lack of training for faculty, and the absence of adequate campus support services (Lewis and Wall, 1988). In this chapter, we address some of these issues.

NEW DIRECTIONS FOR TEACHING AND LEARNING, no. 51, Fall 1992 © Jossey-Bass Publishers

What Is This Mysterious Entity Called
Instructional Technology?

Instructional technology is one of the great secrets of education. Not many people seem to know what it is, including some of those who claim to be instructional technologists. For example, a common conception is that instructional technology refers to the things, or products, used within the context of teaching and learning, such as projectors, films, videocassette players, and perhaps even chalkboards and workbooks. That is, instructional technology is used synonymously with *learning resources.* This particular delimitation explains why most of the persons on college campuses who consider themselves instructional technologists are situated in media centers, where the focus of services is often limited to audiovisual equipment and learning materials. In some circles, the term is used interchangeably with *academic computing.*

Both learning resources and academic computing are essential forms of instructional technology, to be sure, but instructional technology is a much broader concept. Of equal importance to college faculty is its strong emphasis on the processes of teaching. The President's Commission on Instructional Technology (Tickton, 1970, p. 21) defined this perspective as "a systematic way of designing, carrying out, and evaluating *the total process of learning and teaching* [emphasis added] in terms of specific objectives, based on research in human learning and communication, and employing a combination of human and nonhuman resources to bring about more effective instruction." This conception of instructional technology, which evolved in the 1960s, became known as the "systems approach" to instruction, and it was manifested in the process called *instructional development.* While this approach was applied primarily to the development of media-based instructional systems and learning materials, the methodology involved was equally applicable to college courses. In fact, Diamond (1989) recently described applications of the systems approach to course and curriculum development in higher education.

Many different models for the design and implementation of instructional development have evolved over the years, but most have the same basic characteristics. Instructional goals are established. The target student group is analyzed. Student outcomes are determined, in the form of terminal objectives. The information and skills that students are expected to learn are identified and analyzed. Instructional strategies, or lesson plans, are devised. Learning materials are developed. Student assessment measures are written. Formative evaluation instruments are prepared and implemented to identify revision needs, and changes are made as necessary. Summative evaluation is conducted to determine overall effectiveness.

Think now about the process of college teaching. These are events that take place in one form or another in virtually all college courses. Every college professor has some sort of instructional goals, if not objectives, even if they are determined by the textbook table of contents. Every professor has some idea of what to expect from his or her students. Every professor has some means of assessing student performance. Courses are frequently changed in some way from one semester to the next as the result of feedback received by the professor. At the postsecondary level, summative evaluation takes the form of instructor evaluation for the purposes of promotion, tenure, and salary increases.

Instructional development, therefore, takes place in the office of each and every person who teaches a college-level course. Every college faculty member is an instructional developer and, by extension, an instructional technologist. All of the computers, overhead projectors, and videotape players on campus could be pitched into the nearest lake, and instruction could continue, albeit with less effectiveness. But if instructional development were banned, the academy may as well close its doors, because we could not teach without it. This is a powerful realization. Whatever resistance we may harbor toward instructional technology, if we teach at the college level, we are instructional technologists. We are all in this together. We may as well make the best of it.

There is more. According to the Association for Educational Communications and Technology (1977), the major national professional organization in the field, the components of an instructional system include messages, people, materials, devices, techniques, and settings. We have recognized for years that materials and devices are concerns of instructional technology. The association is telling us that so too are the techniques used by professors in the classroom, the professors themselves, and the classrooms. The activities of providing assistance to faculty members in planning courses, preparing individual learning activities, and even developing basic teaching skills are as much instructional technology functions as is pushing a projector cart into the classroom. But these activities are even more important because they go right to the heart of the teaching-learning process.

The early proponents of instructional technology did the field a disservice with their emphasis on large-scale instructional systems, with teams of people working on projects so vast that external, often federal, funding was required. Faculty members and administrators were further intimidated by well-meaning proposals calling for the establishment of complex campus units to support the development of these systems, such as the instructional systems organization model conceptualized by Fraley and Vargas (1975). This model specified separate divisions for curriculum and design, production, instructional operations, quality control, and administration, with the organization staffed by "instructional system technologists whose expertise is to specify how skills and concepts are to be taught, . . . instructional illustrators, narrators, photographers, TV producers, document production specialists, and others expert in producing and acquiring finished and raw materials, . . . facilities management personnel and content knowledgable personnel associated with specific instructional programs, . . . instructional researchers, computer specialists, data processors, and analysts, . . . [and] administrators, system theorists, and instructional technologists" (1975, pp. 8–9). One wonders if this kind of an operation could only have been managed by Cecil B. deMille and funded by the savings and loan industry.

Instructional technology does not have to be complex. It does not have to be expensive. It need not involve a cast of thousands. Instructional technology may take the form of a professor making a few transparencies for a lecture, the retrofitting of a classroom to install a video-data projector, the development of a learning activity to help students use application software in a microcomputer laboratory, the production of a videotape to illustrate a difficult concept, or the presentation of a workshop on facilitating interaction in the classroom.

Use of Technology in the Instructional Context

Knapper (1982b, p. 82) observed that "no technical innovation, no matter how sophisticated, will succeed educationally if it is based upon faulty, or nonexistent, pedagogical foundations." Effective use of technology begins with a well-conceived course, with learning objectives and content carefully selected to meet student needs. Lesson plans and learning activities should be crafted to enable students to meet the course goals. Media, including computing resources, are used as tools by the instructor, or by students, to perform specific tasks in this teaching and learning scheme. We cannot overemphasize the necessity for faculty members to regard media technologies as resources that provide unique learning opportunities for students, within the broader context of a carefully structured learning environment.

What are the roles that media technologies might play? Lewis and Wall (1988, p. 3) identified six reasons frequently cited by faculty members for using these technologies in their teaching:

To accomplish tasks that they cannot do by themselves, such as help students experience times, places, people, and events that cannot be otherwise incorporated into the class.

To accomplish tasks better than they can by themselves, such as help students visualize phenomena that are too small or too dynamic to convey effectively with print or static models or hand waving.

To perform routine teaching tasks which instructors can do but prefer not to, such as helping students overcome individual learning differences through drill and practice.

To prepare students for the world of work, such as how to use and apply spreadsheet, word processing, or computer-aided design technologies.

To enhance faculty and/or student productivity, thereby reducing time required for routine recordkeeping or communication, such as writing or revising or specific teaching or learning styles.

To reach, via distance learning, those students who chose not or are unable to attend classes on campus in the conventional manner.

Another way of looking at the mission of media technology is to consider its functions within a model for teaching, such as the "events of instruction" described by Robert Gagne (Gagne, Briggs, and Wager, 1988). According to Gagne, in an effective instructional unit, the teacher gains the students' attention, informs them of the learning objectives, stimulates recall of appropriate past learning, presents the stimulus information, provides learning guidance, provides practice opportunities followed by appropriate feedback, assesses performance (tests), and provides additional activities to enhance retention and transfer. Media might be used by faculty members to perform specific roles within this model, as in the following examples: (1) To stimulate interest in learning to use the campus library (gaining attention), a videotape made with undergraduate student actors may sensitize new students to the wealth of resources available and demonstrate how easily these resources can be used. The tape could be followed by live instruction that further explains how to use the library and provides students with practice search opportunities. (2) An architecture professor can explain and demonstrate computer-aided design software by projecting the computer output in the classroom (providing learning guidance) and then giving students assignments that require the use of the software in a microcomputer laboratory (practice and feedback). (3) The ability of an educational administration class to use a teaching performance assessment instrument can be tested by having students use the instrument to evaluate a videotaped lesson of an actual classroom teacher (assessing performance).

Need for Support Services

Academic libraries are, of course, universal to college and university campuses. Most institutions also have established centralized media centers and academic computing units. About half of all four-year institutions support active faculty development programs. The mere presence of these services, however, does not mean that they are given adequate funding to function effectively, or that they are able to provide the assistance that faculty require. For example, in a recent national survey, Albright (1991) found startling differences in the funding levels provided to media centers by their institutions (also see Albright, this volume). Many faculty development programs also operate on shoestring budgets. Even academic libraries are now experiencing dramatic budget reductions.

It is unreasonable to expect faculty members to acquire and use technology, or even to become interested in technology, without the presence of active support services. Obstacles blocking the use of technology can and should be addressed by campus instructional support agencies. The most critical support, of course, is to provide the technologies or to assist academic units in their purchase. Of only slightly less importance are consulting services to help faculty members use these technologies effectively in their teaching. Thus, support units need to be staffed by personnel who fully understand the college teaching process, in addition to their own respective areas of technology. The director of each unit, at the very minimum, should have strong academic credentials and the ability to work effectively with faculty members as a consultant and peer.

Support services can promote the effective use of technology in several other ways. Workshops, seminars, individual consultations, and other programs can enlighten faculty about available resources and how to physically operate the equipment, use computer software, create learning materials, and use technology effectively with students. Programs such as these can be very successful in overcoming faculty fears of and misconceptions about technology. As faculty interest grows, it becomes easier to build a consensus for including technology in academic development plans. It is imperative, then, that active collaborative relationships be forged between instructional support units and the authors of documents stating campus goals and priorities. Increased faculty demand for instructional technology also makes it easier to justify funding requests.

Periodic campuswide instructional technology fairs or expositions, sponsored by support units, have proved to be highly successful vehicles for sensitizing faculty to services available and demonstrating the many ways that technology can be used in college teaching. In addition to exhibits showcasing the support services, campus groups with special interests in instructional technology (for example, computer user groups), and local area vendors, most colleges and universities have a cadre of faculty members who are already active users of technology and are willing to set up demonstrations for their faculty colleagues. This peer interaction may be the most valuable feature of these demonstrations. Perhaps the premiere example of an instructional technology fair is the Media Break exposition held annually since 1980 at Iowa State University in Ames. A one-day event, Media Break typically offers thirty to forty exhibits and attracts over five hundred visitors. It has been given much credit for stimulating interest in instructional technology on the Iowa State campus (Albright, 1984).

Where Do We Go from Here?

Although funding for technology acquisition and support services will continue to be a problem, other obstacles (some call them excuses) to the adoption and use of technology in college classrooms will not be valid much longer. Societal pressures alone will mandate that we make significant changes in our approaches to teaching as we near the turn of the century. The "chalk-and-talk" era is just about over for many disciplines. Colleges and universities will have to incorporate technology into their curricula or they simply will not be competitive with institutions that have made the transition.

The students of the 1990s have been surrounded by technology virtually all of their lives. They come to our campuses more technologically literate than many of their professors. Most have cable television, videocassette recorders, and electronic games at home, and many of their families own camcorders and personal computers with access to commercial data bases such as *CompuServe* and *Prodigy*. At the high school level, students are inundated by technology. They use computer laboratories, where they word process, use application software, and communicate with other students around the world via electronic mail networks. They receive the morning news and commentary in their classrooms from the satellite-based Channel One or Turner Educational Services' CNN Newsroom. They have taken high school courses by satellite from Texas Interactive Instructional Network (TI-IN), from Oklahoma State's Arts and Sciences Teleconferencing Service, or from regional or statewide terrestrial networks. They have taken media courses and created their own learning materials in video or multimedia formats. They carry portable cassette and compact disk players everywhere they go, and in their spare time they spend their money in video game parlors. Coming from this electronic world, how can they find appeal in the typical college lecture?

The demands of the marketplace for graduates will also exert heavy pressure on colleges and universities to use technology in their classrooms. In addition to increased expectations for knowledge and skills, employers expect job applicants to be well versed in and comfortable with Information Age technologies, particularly those used in their own work settings. It is a matter of great concern to these employers that education has the lowest capital investment in technology, by far, of any industry in America. While private industry spends an average of $50,000 per employee on technology, the average for education (including K-12) is just $1,000 per employee (Melnick, 1990). Not only does this minimal investment shift much of the burden for job training from the university to the employer, but it results in inefficient use of learning time during students' college years. Almost all productivity gain comes from increased use of technology. Melnick (1990) observed that if the growth of productivity in education had matched the growth of productivity in the computer industry, we would now be able to consolidate twelve years of public education into ten minutes, costing five cents per student. How much longer can higher education afford to offer inefficient instructional programs that do not meet the demands of the marketplace for graduates?

Questions such as these have profound implications for college faculty members in the 1990s. Educational change must begin with the faculty. Only they can make the personal commitments necessary to use technology in their teaching. Only they can exert pressure on administrators and funding agencies to make investment in technology a priority. Only they can demand the provision of a full range of essential support services, including those oriented toward teaching processes and the physical environment for learning.

We are nine years away from the third millenium. If we feel that technology dominates our lives now, we can imagine the impact it will have in the twenty-first century. Institutions that cling to anachronistic teaching practices and attempt to justify them with the same tired old arguments will likely find it increasingly difficult to retain the confidence of legislatures, governing boards, potential employers for graduates, parents, high school seniors and their college counselors, and the general public. Resistance to technology is scarcely worth the price.

References

Albright, M. J. "How to Mount a Successful Media Fair." *Instructional Innovator,* 1984, 29 (7), 23–25.

Albright, M. J. "A Profile of the Profession as We Enter the Last Decade of the Century." Paper presented at the annual spring conference of the Consortium of College and University Media Centers, Philadelphia, May 1991.

Association for Educational Communications and Technology. *The Definition of Educational Technology.* Washington, D.C.: Association for Educational Communications and Technology, 1977.

Diamond, R. M. *Designing and Improving Courses and Curricula in Higher Education: A Systematic Approach.* San Francisco: Jossey-Bass, 1989.

Fraley, L. E., and Vargas, E. A. "Academic Tradition and Instructional Technology." *Journal of Higher Education,* 1975, 45 (1), 1–15.

Gagne, R. M., Briggs, L. J., and Wager, W. W. *Principles of Instructional Design.* (3rd ed.) Troy, Mo.: Holt, Rinehart & Winston, 1988.

Green, K. C. "A Technology Agenda for the 1990s." *Change,* 1991, 23 (1), 6–7.

Knapper, C. K. "Editor's Notes." In C. K. Knapper (ed.), *Expanding Learning Through New Communications Technologies.* New Directions for Teaching and Learning, no. 9. San Francisco: Jossey-Bass, 1982a.

Knapper, C. K. "Technology and Teaching: Future Prospects." In C. K. Knapper (ed.), *Expanding Learning Through New Communications Technologies.* New Directions for Teaching and Learning, no. 9. San Francisco: Jossey-Bass, 1982b.

Lewis, R. J., and Wall, M. *Exploring Obstacles to Uses of Technology in Higher Education: A Discussion Paper.* Washington, D.C.: Academy for Educational Development, 1988.

McNeil, D. R. "Status of Technology in Higher Education: A Reassessment." Paper presented at the 2nd annual conference on Interactive Technology and Telecommunications, Augusta, Maine, September 1988.

Melnick, R. "Education, Media, and the Future." Paper presented at the Managing Media for Change Institute, San Francisco, May 1990.

Tickton, S. G. *To Improve Learning: An Evaluation of Instructional Technology.* New York: Bowker, 1970.

MICHAEL J. ALBRIGHT is director of the Center for Instructional Support, University of Hawaii at Manoa, Honolulu.

DAVID L. GRAF is coordinator for instructional development at the Media Resources Center, Iowa State University, Ames.

State-of-the-art presentation graphics systems are an essential component of a long-range strategy designed to change the teaching-learning paradigm.

New Directions in Presentation Graphics: Impact on Teaching and Learning

J. Thomas Head

> To envision information—and what bright and splendid visions can result—is to work at the intersection of image, word, number, art.
>
> —Tufte, 1990, p. 9

This chapter examines the implications of computer-generated presentation graphics for the teaching-learning process. In this context, teaching-learning is not restricted to the traditional classroom setting but rather includes all situations related to learning, both formal and informal. Thus, the ideas discussed here are relevant to presentations at professional meetings, research seminars, continuing education short courses, computer-aided instruction, and traditional lectures. In addition, the hardware and software of state-of-the-art presentation graphics are described along with the future trends in this rapidly changing technology.

As a point of departure, the following definitions (Pfaffenberger, 1990) serve to clarify the focus of discussion in this chapter: *Analytical graphics* are charts and graphs that aid a professional in the interpretation of data. These graphics are usually generated using computer software such as spreadsheets, data bases, and scientific visualization packages. *Presentation graphics* are charts and graphs that are enhanced to be visually appealing and easily understood by the audience, such as text charts, business graphics (bar and line graphs and pie charts), and the more sophisticated scientific graphs, maps, and pictorial images used in the academic disciplines. These graphics are generated either by importing data from analytical software or through direct input by the user.

Presentation Graphics in the University

The design of presentation graphics for the teaching-learning process has traditionally been a complex and demanding task. Under pressure to prepare materials for lectures and conference presentations, faculty typically have used illegible graphics that detract from rather than enhance otherwise carefully prepared presentations (MacGregor, 1979). The only recourse for faculty members lacking natural talent in graphics design, and even for faculty with this talent, has been to use the services of professional graphic designers either in a centralized campus service or in commercial services off-campus. This has often required long lead times and involved expensive corrections and unsatisfactory end results.

As hardware costs continue to drop and software developers increase the power and ease of use of presentation graphics products, the ability to design effective materials for teaching and conference presentations is now within the reach of all faculty. Users who are willing to commit the necessary time and energy will find that the computer graphics systems available today facilitate the production of these materials. The ability to display complex relationships within a wide variety of disciplines is finally within the grasp of all who have a minimum of computer skills. Since the cost of these systems has dropped dramatically in the past several years, it is now possible for practically everyone to gain access to the hardware and software needed to create effective presentation graphics materials. Even those who still decide to use the services of professional designers will see major improvements in the quality of materials due to the increased productivity and creative power of the designer working on a computer graphics workstation.

It is already apparent in the corporate sector that presentations have changed dramatically because of presentation graphics systems. In this fast-paced business environment, it is essential that complex relationships be communicated as efficiently and effectively as possible in presentations. It is no longer acceptable to rely on mediocre graphics materials. Whether displaying sales projections or market trends, presenters are using high-quality materials prepared on their own workstations with data imported from spreadsheets or data bases. Similarly, in the increasingly competitive university environment, faculty are using these systems to enhance their teaching and conference presentations and their proposals in the competition for research dollars.

Presentation Process

An analysis of the process used to prepare materials for teaching and conference presentations yields the following steps, regardless of media format:

Conceptualization. Prior to the creation of presentation materials, faculty members must determine what types of materials are relevant to the concepts that they are teaching. This step in the process generally occurs prior to any interaction with graphic designers or photographers. A faculty member may seek the assistance of a consultant to determine the feasibility of creating a particular type of image.

Creation. The creation of a professional quality image usually requires the assistance of a consultant such as a graphic designer or photographer who has expertise in using the tools of the trade to translate an idea into a rough draft.

Production. Production of the final image traditionally has required the technical expertise of specialists in each of the separate technologies such as photography and graphic arts. The artist produces the final version of the materials using graphics software, and the photographer uses cameras and film processing to complete the project.

Distribution. Presentation materials such as 35mm slides and overhead transparencies are distributed to faculty members from centralized facilities for use in classrooms and seminars.

Utilization. Images are shown on projection screens for the purpose of enhancing the quality of the communication process by explicating complex topics in teaching and research presentations.

Presentation Technology

Over the past decade, there have been dramatic advances in the technology used to prepare presentation materials (Head and Lockwood, 1989). Figure 2.1 shows the traditional model for using analog image technologies in the production of presentation materials. Each of these separate technologies is independent and irreversible. These include traditional photographic production methods, graphic arts techniques using pen and ink, and related technologies, all of which involve a high degree of technical skill and experience. With these traditional technologies, the task of making changes to the images usually requires starting the entire process from the beginning, which adds costs in terms of time and materials.

However, the introduction of digital technology to the production process has provided a new model. Figure 2.2 illustrates a model based on digital image technologies. Digital technology is allowing a transition from irreversible to reversible production processes. A computer graphics image can be edited electronically, an electronic photograph can be enhanced by

**Figure 2.1. Traditional Model of Analog Image
Technologies in the Presentation Process**

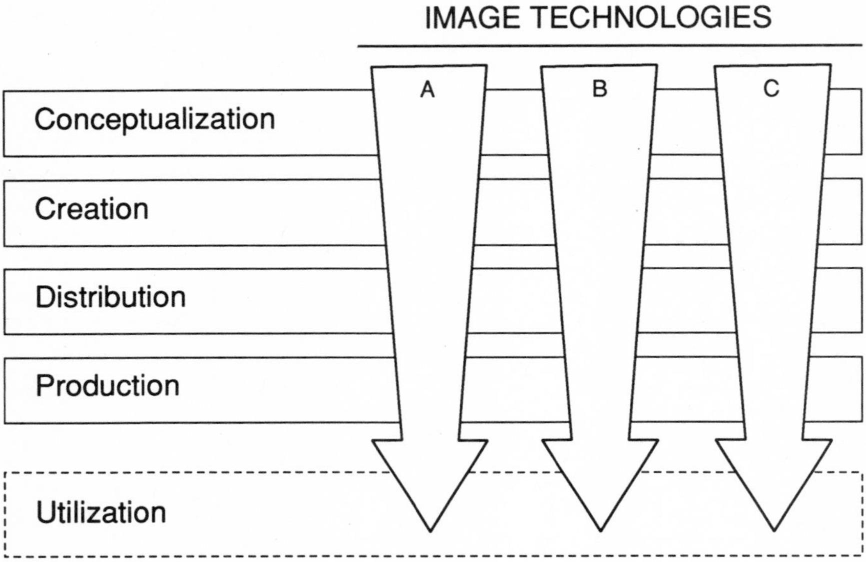

image-processing software, and a page layout of a publication can be modified prior to final production in hard copy format. These kinds of modifications mean that the order of the steps in the imaging process also can be altered.

Specifically, the order of production and distribution in some cases may be reversed because it is easier and more economical to distribute the image electronically for display in the new environment. A hard copy may be produced on the site of the final utilization, or it may never be produced at all. Thus, it is possible for faculty and students from a wide variety of disciplines to conceptualize images, create them in a local environment, and then distribute them through electronic networks on campus or across the country for production in various forms. In summary, production, distribution, and utilization are interchangeable components in the process, which remains reversible until the last possible moment. The effects of this new technology have significantly enhanced the effectiveness and productivity of the entire process.

Electronic Studio

The long-term strategy of media production units is the establishment of state-of-the-art electronic studios to serve the needs of faculty members. The electronic studio is conceived as a way to make centralized production

**Figure 2.2. Digital Model of Image Technologies
in the Presentation Process**

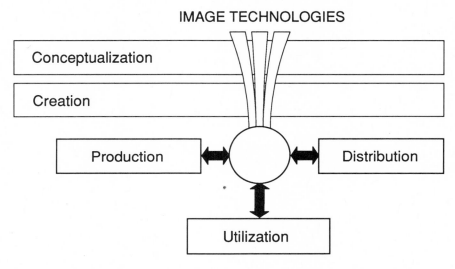

services and human assistance as readily available as possible in the user's own environment. The studio would accept information in a wide variety of formats, transform that information into the appropriate media format using professional design skills, and provide high-quality output (Davis, 1989). The production services include computer-generated 35mm slides and overhead transparencies, scanning services, color laser copies, film processing and printing, camera-ready text and graphics, and high-speed copying, printing, and binding. The goal is to make the production and distribution of presentation materials available on local networks. This goal involves such devices as remotely driven film recorders available twenty-four hours a day and electronic distribution of images to high-resolution display devices in the classroom. Figure 2.3 shows an idealized electronic studio environment that would make these resources more readily available at the desktop. The two major impediments to implementation of the electronic studio environment are the size of image files and the lack of file compatibility due to still evolving standards.

Image File Size. One of the major problems associated with a digital production environment is the size of files generated by the scanning of continuous tone images and full-motion video. The rapid development and adoption of standards for compressing files will expedite the implementation of this goal on college campuses. In addition, the completion of fiber-optic networks will substantially alleviate many of the problems of file size.

Figure 2.3. Electronic Studio Environment

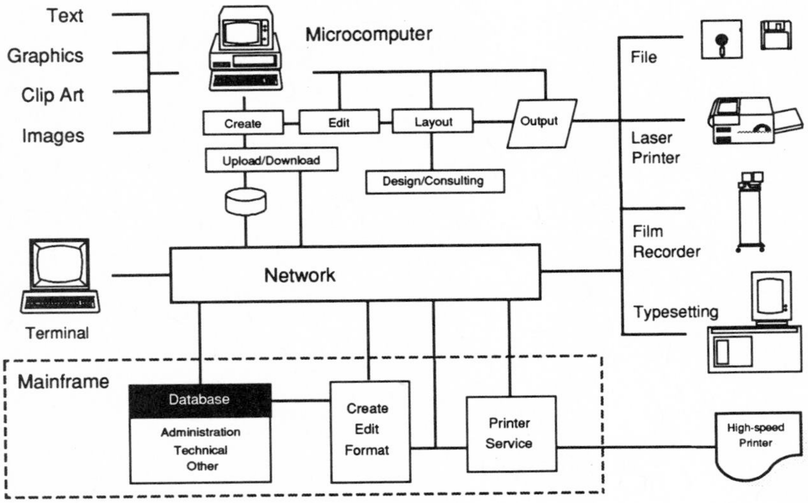

Standards. The evolution of standards such as Standard Generalized Markup Language and the Computer Graphics Metafile will provide improved flexibility in file interchange. Although incompatibility of standards still presents problems in the actual production environment, tremendous strides have been made that greatly enhance compatibility and bring us closer to realizing the goal of full compatibility across all possible standards.

Implications for Teaching and Learning

Faculty members have been aware of the desirability of using graphics to explain complex relationships but have been deterred by the difficulties of communicating with graphic artists, the long turnaround times, and the cost. The current technology allows faculty to experiment with new ideas and make last-minute changes while controlling the cost of these changes, even if a professional graphic designer is involved in putting the finishing touches on the presentation.

In general, high-quality presentation graphics provide three major benefits to the user in the teaching environment: gaining and maintaining attention, efficiency, and effectiveness (Wileman, 1980). More specifically, the benefits include clarification of complex relationships, summary of large masses of data, provision of a comprehensive picture of a problem, and exposure of hidden facts and spatial relationships that stimulate analytical thinking and promote class discussion (Schmid and Schmid, 1979). The power of computer graphics allows faculty members to experiment with new ways of explaining complex topics and to modify the graphic images to meet the needs of their students based on their experience in the classroom.

Today's students are constantly bombarded with high-quality media materials. The explosion of information available in the teaching situation requires faculty to design materials that are cost-effective and yet provide insights into complex relationships in this rapidly changing environment. The most effective application of presentation graphics is the use of still and animated sequences to explicate concepts that cannot be explained purely through the verbal mode. For example, aided by computers that convert large data banks into images on a screen, scientists are able to see everything from living cells to individual atoms in three-dimensional, photo-realistic color (Nash, 1991). These images are then stored in computer files for eventual output to the appropriate device for teaching and research presentations. The effectiveness of these presentations is dramatically improved because the presenter can display relevant images without being at the mercy of traditional labor-intensive production methods. The computer-generated images are more readily available as hard copy or electronic images because of the rapid advances in output and display devices.

With the increasing emphasis on productivity in teaching, it is essential to adopt these methods during these times of shrinking resources. With the increasing competition for students on college campuses and the renewed emphasis on teaching excellence from parents, boards, and legislators, it is essential that faculty improve the quality of instructional materials. These improvements will require increased support for hardware and software systems as well as consultants to assist faculty in the effective use of these systems.

While the effects of graphics materials on learning are well documented (Winn, 1987), it is helpful to have a conceptual model to assist in interpreting this abundant literature and adapting the findings to specific learning situations. The image classification model serves this dual purpose by clarifying the conceptual basis of stimuli created through presentation graphics technology (Head and Sanders, 1988). The model describes three broad categories that encompass the types of images used in the university environment, as shown in Figure 2.4 (Knowlton, 1966; Wileman, 1980): (1) *Pictorial* images resemble the reality for which they stand; these can range from realistic, full-color renditions of persons, places, or things, to more abstract line drawings that still depict the referent in a realistic manner.[1] (2) *Graphic* images may use arbitrary symbols, but the pattern and/or order of connection of the elements is somehow isomorphic with reality; these include graphs, schematic diagrams, maps, and depictions of abstract rela-

**Figure 2.4. Image Classification Model
for the University Environment**

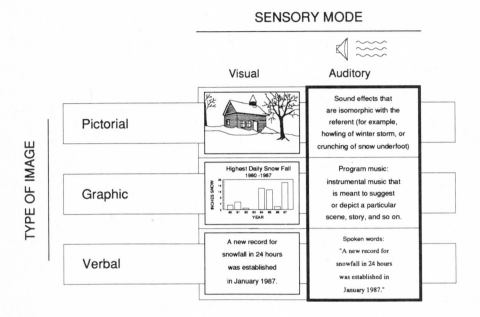

tionships.[2] (3) *Verbal* images use totally arbitrary symbols that by definition do not resemble in any way the reality for which they stand; these include words, numbers, and other arbitrary symbols that are meaningful only to individuals familiar with them.[3]

The types of image, sensory mode, and degree of realism are the stimulus variables that have been shown to have the greatest effect on learning. The amount and quality of feedback to the learner are also important variables affecting learning (Levie and Dickie, 1973; Dwyer, 1978). As multimedia presentations on computers assume an increasingly important role in the teaching-learning process, the power of combining all of these variables in a creative fashion based on learning principles has great potential to improve learning.

The media format, such as 35mm slides and overhead transparencies, has not generally been shown to affect learning (Clark, 1983). Choices of format are primarily practical decisions based on such variables as cost, size of the audience, and style of the presenter.

Media Formats

Although the demise of hard copy presentation media has been predicted for the last several years, the growth in slide and overhead volume continues at a rapid pace. The percentage of materials that will be computer generated is predicted to double over the next two to three years.

35mm Slides. The 35mm color slide remains a major format for presentations by faculty and students in teaching and research activities. Prior to the introduction of digital technology, this process was labor-intensive, requiring tedious photographic copying of hand-drawn graphics materials, processing of black-and-white negatives, and reproduction on color film. This process was plagued with a multitude of production problems related to quality control, limitations on the number of colors that could be reproduced on a single slide, and frequent reshooting of negatives. The introduction of computer-generated graphics with the final output on digital film recorders has greatly enhanced productivity by making it essentially a one-step process (Figure 2.5). In addition, up to sixteen million colors are available, quality-control problems are minimized, and labor costs are drastically reduced.

Overhead Transparencies. The eight-by-ten-inch overhead transparency is used for more informal instructional settings and small meetings. The desktop laser printer driven by a microcomputer or the mainframe has moved this medium from the graphics shop into the hands of the user.

Figure 2.5. Slide Production Process: Old Labor-Intensive Approach Versus New Computer-Generated Graphics Approach

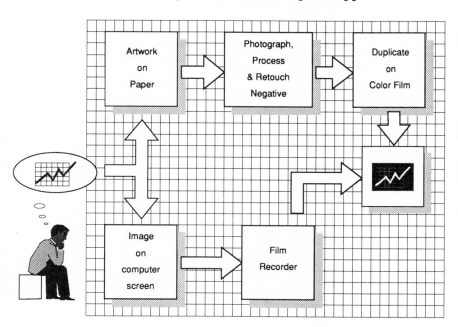

Centralized services may still provide full-color overheads in the short run because of the current cost of color printers. However, the resolution of these printers is much lower than that of the film recorders used to generate 35mm slides. Full-color overheads in the eight-by-ten format can be produced on high-end film recorders at high resolution, but the cost of materials for this large format is prohibitive when compared to 35mm slides.

Electronic Images. The direct display of electronic images using computer-driven liquid crystal display (LCD) pads or video projectors continues to grow in popularity. The color LCD pad is a rapidly changing technology that holds great promise for the teaching environment. While these devices eliminate the production of hard copy media materials, the relatively high cost of these projection devices and limitations on resolution has placed some restrictions on their widespread use. The recent perfection of the blue light emitting diode (LED) should speed up the development of large, flat-screen projection systems. This technology could provide the breakthrough needed for widespread use of electronic image projection in the next several years.

Guideline for Presentation Materials

In order to assist faculty members who are designing their own materials, guidelines for the design of computer-generated presentation materials are given below (Rabb, 1990):

Legibility. Text height should be a minimum of 2 percent of the height of the total image. A larger text size (5 to 10 percent of height) is recommended for better legibility and impact. Use a sans serif font such as Helvetica or Swiss.

Color. Use white or yellow text colors on dark backgrounds such as blue, green, or black. Avoid the use of exotic or garish colors, which are often selected for the sake of variety.

Chart Selection. The versatility provided by the software has made it possible to present numerical information in a multitude of chart formats. Most software packages allow the user to readily display the same data in a variety of different formats with a few simple keystrokes. While empirical data on chart selection are somewhat limited (Head and Moore, 1989), there are general guidelines for the use of the basic types of charts (MacGregor, 1979):

Line Charts. Use these charts to show trends or movement rather than actual amounts, to illustrate a long series of complex data or to compare series of data, and to interpolate or extrapolate.

Semi-Log Line Charts. Use these charts to show relative change when the baseline quantities differ greatly.

Vertical Bar Charts. Use these charts to compare amounts or to emphasize differences in one variable at various periods of time.

Clustered Bar Charts. Use these charts to compare independent series of data over a period of time. The number of bars per cluster should be limited to three.

Stacked Bar Charts. Use these charts to compare totals or sums of totals over a period of time.

Horizontal Bar Charts. Use these charts to compare amounts or emphasize differences at one period of time.

Pie Charts. Use these charts to compare relations of component parts.

Simplicity of Design. Even though computer graphics systems provide a great number of options, including a wide range of color choices, always keep in mind that simplicity is the goal of design. When the highest-quality presentation is required, it may still be necessary for many users to employ the services of a professional graphic designer. Even the clip art or templates provided in the software packages may need refinement in order to meet the needs of specific teaching situations.

Presentation Graphics Software

The current software packages available for preparation of presentation graphics materials represent a highly developed technology that can provide substantial benefits to even the casual user. These packages have been designed to supplement word processors, spreadsheets, and statistical analysis packages, which traditionally have lacked flexibility in formatting, to create high-quality, effective presentation materials. The current trend is to include templates for text charts, chart galleries for numerical data, and clip art for pictorial concepts. Other enhancements include outliners for organization of presentations, electronic slide sorting, and printing of speaker notes and audience handouts. All of the charts, handouts, and notes are stored in a single computer file (Fridlund, 1991).

Today's software is a vast improvement over the earlier software packages, which were relatively difficult to learn and, overall, were not an efficient way for faculty to spend their time either in learning the software or in producing their presentations. This inefficiency often led to some very poorly designed presentations by early users, who were unprepared to deal with the multitude of decisions regarding text size, color selection, chart formatting, and illustration of concepts required to use the earlier versions of these packages.

The following is a summary of the features that are incorporated in most of the current software packages and should be helpful in evaluating and selecting the appropriate package (Green and Green, 1992).

Outliners and Text Treatment. This feature allows the user to organize the presentation in outline form and then to place the text into a template. Usually, these templates are "smart" in that changes made to the text in the individual slides are reflected in the outline.

Templates. These are either professionally designed backgrounds and formats that are included with the software or have been designed and or modified by users to meet their own specific needs. Templates provide consistency in presentation since color selections, fonts, logos, and other graphic elements are maintained throughout the series of slides. Templates also provide the correct ratios for output as overhead transparencies, 35mm slides, or electronic displays.

Graphics. The relative importance of the ability to create graphic elements depends on the graphic design capabilities of the user. Most presentation packages do not provide the advanced features available in packages designed for professional illustrators but are usually adequate for most users. The clip art provided can assist the casual user who lacks artistic ability.

Charts and Graphs. This feature provides automatic generation of graphs and tables from numerical data, with the capability to select the type of graph from a chart gallery. The best packages allow users to modify the graphs as needed to meet their own specific needs.

Notes and Handouts. Most packages now provide the capability to print speaker notes and audience handouts. This feature allows the user to prepare a complete presentation, with materials that help to reinforce the message after the audience has dispersed.

Slide-Show Features and Effects. Computer projection systems have made it easier for the presenter to use electronic images, which can be enhanced with special transition effects. These systems also allow the user to go to a specific slide at random without having to shuttle through a tray of conventional slides.

Import-Export Output. The ability to import and export text, graphics, and numerical files is essential for productivity. Be sure to check that the software supports output devices that can generate the types of materials needed for the presentation.

Overall Ease of Use. Many of the current packages are designed for the occasional user who does not want to spend an inordinate amount of time learning the software. The more advanced software will, of course, provide additional capabilities and a longer learning curve.

System Components

In order to be productive while working on a graphics workstation, there are hardware requirements that go beyond those needed for basic word processing. The basic components of a presentation graphics system are a relatively fast microcomputer, a high-capacity disk storage system, a high-resolution display, and a printer. It is also desirable to have access to a scanner and to high-resolution output devices for color. Many major university media operations now provide these high-resolution output services for their faculty members.[4]

Trends in Presentation Graphics

The trends in presentation graphics are increasing processor speed, higher-resolution displays, and easier-to-use software with expanded clip art libraries and high-quality templates. The future lies in the electronic display of still and motion images through computer display devices, which gives the presenter greater flexibility in the design, creation, and adaptation of the presentation to meet the needs of the audience. As discussed earlier, the goal is to keep the images in digital electronic form as long as possible and, except in unusual circumstances, not to produce hard copy at all. This approach allows editing of the image at the last possible moment or even "on the fly" depending on the learning situation. The introduction of multimedia presentations incorporating full-motion video, sound, and animated sequences finally gives the instructor the power for real breakthroughs in the teaching-learning paradigm.

During the 1990s, institutions and individual faculty members should be getting ready for the expected changes in the teaching-learning paradigm. The renewed emphasis on teaching excellence in universities, demands for increased accountability for the education of undergraduate students, and declining budgets resulting in larger class sizes make the continued use of mediocre teaching materials unacceptable. It behooves institutions to provide the resources to faculty members that will enable them to be competitive both in the classroom and in their research endeavors. The challenge is to stay abreast of these rapidly changing technologies in the 1990s in order to take advantage of new paradigms such as computer-based instruction, distance learning, and the education of nontraditional students.

Developing Technologies

The following rapidly emerging technologies have implications for presentation graphics even though some have limitations in terms of cost, speed, and quality control.

Electronic Photography. Until very recently, electronic photography was in analog form. The cameras were miniature videocassette recorders that captured a series of still images on floppy disk, limiting the resolution to the quality of broadcast television, which is not acceptable for printing technology and of minimal usefulness in presentations. However, experimental digital still cameras are beginning to hit the marketplace. The size of the image files will remain a problem until image compression algorithms that can operate on the fly are more readily available.

Desktop Video. The introduction of desktop video is one of the most exciting developments in recent years. This development will have a dramatic impact on how we communicate. Software and hardware are emerging that enable users to edit and display video sequences on their personal work-stations, a capability that has great potential for enhancing the teaching-learning process. Through a combination of video and computer-animated sequences, this technology can improve the communication of complex concepts that cannot be easily grasped through use of still images. These video sequences may now be incorporated into on-screen presentations (Borzo, 1992) and even into traditional text documents.

Multimedia. Multimedia presentations generated and displayed through microcomputers constitute a rapidly developing technology. Multipurpose audiovisual boards will provide flexibility in the design of self-contained presentations and instructional activities and should prove to be effective in a wide variety of settings. This hardware enables users to capture and edit sound and images, create special effects, and produce interactive presentations. In addition to image editing, drawing, and colorization, high-resolution text can be superimposed along with digitized sound for voice, music, and sound effects—a capability that has the potential to revolutionize the communication process in business and education. The complexity of designing multimedia presentations will be a deterrent to widespread production by faculty members without assistance from experts in the field. However, the graphics prepared using the simpler presentation packages can still be incorporated into these more complex programs.

The challenge is to use the technology to change the teaching-learning paradigm. The technology will continue to improve. The only potential limitation in the long run is our level of commitment to use it creatively in our efforts to enhance instruction.

Notes

1. This type of image is usually stored in the computer as a bit map, which, depending on the resolution and color depth of the scan, can consume up to one megabyte per square inch. This consumption rate presents storage problems unless removable cartridges or optical media are used. However, the rapidly developing compression algorithms such as the JPEG standard should help to alleviate this problem. These compression techniques can compress files in ratios of up to 20:1 without significant losses in quality.

2. This type of image is stored in the computer as a set of objects, which presents a much lower demand on storage space and can usually be stored on standard devices such as hard disks or even floppy disks. Another advantage is the high quality of output available from these object-based files.

3. These symbols for most documents can be stored as ASCII code, which presents the lowest demand for storage space and allows large amounts of text data to be stored on standard storage devices.

4. In the disk-operated system (DOS) environment, a 25-MHz microcomputer and a 640-by-480 display is the minimum configuration for efficient production of presentation graphics. A windows-based software package provides greater ease of learning and use, although some of the older DOS-based software packages still provide high-quality materials with a somewhat steeper learning curve. Most of the DOS software has been or will be soon ported to Windows, which provides a more productive environment for presentation graphics software.

An Apple Macintosh of comparable speed and resolution would provide the minimum hardware requirement for presentations. This platform provides the usual advantages of ease of use and other advantages attributed to this environment. The current trend is to make the most popular presentation software packages available on both platforms.

The multitasking capability of high-end workstations operating in the UNIX environment provides significant advantages for presentation design where the integration of text, graphics, and realistic pictorial images is required. These workstations can also function as file servers to store archival images in departmental files.

The new personal scanners and enhanced printers provide a good system for capturing images on the fly and incorporating them into presentations at the last minute. The price-performance curve for desktop color scanners is becoming attractive to even casual users. This trend, along with the standardization of compression algorithms, will permit the incorporation of realistic, full-color images on a routine basis.

References

Borzo, J. "Persuasion Upgrade for Mac Released." *Infoworld,* 1992, *14* (1), 14.

Clark, R. E. "The Next Decade of Instructional Technology Research." *Educational Considerations,* 1983, *10* (2), 33–35.

Davis, L. M. *Toward the Electronic Studio.* Washington, D.C.: Davis, 1989.

Dwyer, F. M. *Strategies for Improving Visual Learning.* State College, Pa.: Learning Services, 1978.

Fridlund, A. J. "Presentations Graphics for DOS and Windows." *Infoworld,* 1991, *13* (37), 61–76.

Green, D., and Green, D. "Attention Part-Time Presenters." *Publish,* 1992, *7* (2), 72–78.

Head, J. T., and Lockwood, A. F. *A Unified Plan for Media Production Services.* Blacksburg: Information Systems, Virginia Polytechnic Institute and State University, 1989.

Head, J. T., and Moore, D. M. "The Effect of Graphic Format on the Interpretation of Quantitative Data." *Journal of Educational Technology Systems,* 1989, *17* (4), 337–343.

Head, J. T., and Sanders, W. H. *Task Force on Imagery Research and Transmission.* Blacksburg: Information Systems, Virginia Polytechnic Institute and State University, 1988.

Knowlton, J. Q. "On the Definition of 'Picture.'" *AV Communication Review,* 1966, *14* (2), 157–183.

Levie, W. H., and Dickie, K. E. "The Analysis and Application of Media." In R.M.W. Travers (ed.), *The Second Handbook of Research on Teaching.* Skokie, Ill.: Rand McNally, 1973.

MacGregor, A. J. *Graphics Simplified.* Toronto, Canada: University of Toronto Press, 1979.

Nash, J. M. "Adventures in Lilliput." *Time,* 1991, *138* (26), 75–76.

Pfaffenberger, B. *Que's Computer User's Dictionary.* Carmel, Ind.: Que Corporation, 1990.

Rabb, M. Y. *The Presentation Design Book.* Chapel Hill, N.C.: Ventana Press, 1990.

Schmid, C. F., and Schmid, S. E. *Handbook of Graphic Presentation.* New York: Wiley, 1979.

Tufte, E. R. *Envisioning Information.* Cheshire, Conn.: Graphics Press, 1990.

Wileman, R. E. *Exercises in Visual Thinking.* New York: Hastings House, 1980.

Winn, B. "Charts, Graphs, and Diagrams in Educational Materials." In D. M. Willows and H. A. Houghton (eds.), *The Psychology of Illustration.* Vol. 1: *Basic Research.* New York: Springer-Verlag, 1987.

J. THOMAS HEAD is director of media services at Virginia Polytechnic Institute and State University, Blacksburg.

*Multimedia, a computer-based system incorporating video, audio,
and digital storage media, provides educators with the tools to
bring learning alive for students of all ages. With strategic planning, adequate funding, and faculty development, multimedia may
become the most common form of instructional technology by the
late 1990s.*

Multimedia and the Teaching-Learning Process in Higher Education

Annette C. Lamb

Multimedia is a form of instructional technology that will change the way
many of us think about college teaching. All of the instructional tools that
have appeared in the past two centuries, from textbooks and chalkboards
to slide projectors, videotape players, and computers, are now being merged
into self-contained, interactive workstations. The classrooms of tomorrow
will feature interactive presentation stations linked to wide area networks
that convey audio, video, and data to students both on- and off-site.
Indeed, electronic classrooms such as these have already been developed
on many campuses.

Multimedia classrooms can provide a stimulating environment for
teaching and learning. The most obvious benefit is that a virtually limitless
array of resources can be incorporated into the lesson plan, providing
learning experiences that otherwise would be unavailable to students. Because multiple channels are involved, instructors can address individual
learning styles. Multimedia encourages exploration, self-expression, and a
feeling of ownership by allowing students to manipulate its components.
Active multimedia learning environments foster communication, cooperation, and collaboration among instructor and students. Multimedia makes
learning stimulating, engaging, and fun.

The term *multimedia* was once used to describe combinations of media
formats such as slide projectors and audiotape players. These low-end
systems are still in use and have been greatly enhanced by the availability
of computer graphics, film recorders, and other new production tools.
Multimedia can now be defined as organized access to text (words and
numbers), aural (sound effects, music, and speech), and visual (still images,

NEW DIRECTIONS FOR TEACHING AND LEARNING, no. 51, Fall 1992 © Jossey-Bass Publishers

video, and animation) elements, synthesized into a single, integrated presentation system controlled by a computer.

Components of Multimedia

A microcomputer is at the heart of a multimedia production or presentation system. Various peripheral devices may be added for storage of information that can be retrieved as necessary by users of the system.

Computer. The evolution of powerful, easy-to-use microcomputers, capable of accessing, combining, and controlling multiple sources of information, made possible the development of advanced multimedia technology. The computer acts as the nerve center, selecting and displaying information according to user commands. Both Macintosh and IBM and compatible computers using Windows software provide a graphical user interface that is essential for multimedia displays. This interface not only permits multiple images on the computer screen but also enables users to manipulate those images using a hand-controlled mouse or even "touch-screen" display systems.

Authoring tools, such as HyperCard and IBM Linkway, are easy to learn and can be used by faculty members to develop and present multimedia materials without the need for sophisticated programming skills. General purpose languages such as C are sometimes used to develop special routines that are beyond the capabilities of authoring systems. Multimedia developers can also create, save, modify, and display images using computer graphics software. Networking software is used when multimedia systems are controlled off-site.

Video. Videotape recorders were among the first media forms to be linked with microcomputers for multimedia delivery. These were cumbersome systems because the linear nature of videotape did not permit easy random access. The introduction of laserdisks, which provided easy and quick random access to motion video segments, was a major step forward in multimedia technology. Constant angular velocity (CAV) videodisks provide a medium for storage of up to fifty-four thousand still images or about thirty minutes of video on each side, any of which can be accessed almost instantly. Video compression techniques now permit the storage of video segments on compact disks (CDs) and even on the hard drive of the computer.

Live video may also be part of a multimedia system. A video camera can provide image magnification as part of a demonstration table for scientific applications. For example, live shots of objects, models, or microscopic organisms can be projected simultaneously with prerecorded video segments or computer-generated data.

Audio. Until recently, the audio channel in computer-based instruction was used primarily for reinforcement. The introduction of digital audio, which can record, store, edit, and play back segments of audio precisely and reliably, made possible the effective integration of synchronized, randomly accessed audio into multimedia instruction (Barron, 1991). As with video, audio may require a significant amount of storage space, depending on the amount and complexity of sound required. Audio compact disk players and other peripherals such as musical instrument digital interface (MIDI) devices are sometimes included in multimedia systems.

Digital Storage Media. Digital storage media are now common components of multimedia systems. Introduced in the mid-1980s, compact disk-read only memory (CD-ROM) is used for the storage of digital data, including images, sound, and text. A single CD-ROM can store 650 megabytes of data, more than the entire contents of an encyclopedia. Digital Video Interactive (DVI) is a newer development with exciting potential for multimedia. DVI uses a special chip to compress video, allowing up to seventy-two minutes of video, ten thousand still photographs, one-hundred thousand words, or seventeen hours of audio on a single disk. Video digitizers, scanners, and high-level graphics packages enable multimedia developers to create and store sophisticated color still images, as well as animation.

Additional Components. Display units are a primary concern in the development and delivery of multimedia. Depending on the number of students requiring simultaneous access and the complexity of the multimedia images, display devices can be one or more data-compatible television monitors for small groups, and either multiscan video projectors or liquid crystal display (LCD) panels, used with overhead projectors, for larger groups. Some of these devices have special pointers, light pens, or touch screens for individual interaction or speaker emphasis. Quality audio speakers are also important in a multimedia presentation system. Stereo headphones may be used in independent study and small group settings.

Interactive Multimedia Learning Environments

Multimedia technology has made possible *nonlinear* access to information, providing an active learning environment for thinking, learning, and communication. In a hypermedia, or nonlinear, environment, information is organized in nodes and connected by links. Authoring tools allow multimedia developers to organize and connect information, using nodes and links, to anticipate a variety of paths that students might take toward learning the material being taught, or to consider alternative outcomes to decisions made.

Hypermedia environments may be organized in a number of ways. Some systems contain a mainline of information that is organized in a chronological or alphabetical manner. Other systems may be developed as hierarchies or webs. For example, a history resource may allow students to access information alphabetically, numerically, or chronologically. Students may also be able to access information by political issue, by geographical location, or by subject. While one user may seek still images of clothing for a fashion history project, another student may use the same resource for a project dealing with political issues in a presidential campaign. Each may encounter graphics, audio, still images, and motion video segments related to his or her area of interest. Such interactivity encourages problem solving and invites individually customized, inquiry-driven approaches to learning (Nicol, 1988).

The combination of multimedia and hypermedia makes learning an active process. Students use technology to communicate ideas in a learning environment that stresses a constructive, rather than instructive, approach. In the past, the developer, disseminator, and user were three discrete elements of a multimedia package. According to Pea (1991, p. 58), "Whereas movies separate directors and viewers, the technology of interactive multimedia can unite creators and viewers in much the same way as the technology of writing unites writers and readers. Society might come to regard multimedia literacy as essential as writing is today."

For example, in response to industry's demand for employees with skills in teamwork and collaboration, faculty members at Cornell University turned to multimedia to create collaborative design environments. A multimedia network enables engineering students to exchange engineering design options and other information as part of project development assignments (Gay and Thomas, 1992). Proponents of learning experiences such as these see three important benefits. First, a hypermedia environment provides flexibility and ease of use. Information is networked rather than presented in a linear fashion. Second, because hypermedia materials are more engaging than traditional print materials, learners spend more time processing information. And, third, students have increased motivation when using hypermedia materials because they are in control (Carlson, 1990).

This approach to learning has been criticized by those who believe that students do not always make wise decisions about their own learning. Tennyson (1981) and others have found that students make better decisions about their own learning when an advisory function is incorporated into hypermedia environments. Lamb and Myers (1990) advocated the use of a mentor system designed to give students control of their learning environment without becoming overwhelmed and frustrated. This approach is used with chemistry students at the University of Illinois at Urbana-Champaign. Simulated reality and tutorials give students the freedom to explore chemical systems, while at the same time monitoring progress and providing context-sensitive help (Jones and Smith, 1992).

Numerous studies (for example, Bationo, 1991; Nasser and McEwen, 1976; Strang, 1973) have concluded that the use of multiple sensory channels is more effective than the use of each alone. The "cue summation" principle suggests that a combination of channels offers learners a variety of visual and auditory cues, so each learner is able to select the best cues to meet his or her individual sensory needs. According to Strang (1973), since each person's "environmental receptivity" differs, opportunities should be provided for each person to match his or her sensory preferences to available resources. Multimedia materials provide these opportunities.

Miller (1990) summarized ten additional benefits of interactive technologies: (1) More than thirty studies have found that interactive technologies reduce learning time. (2) Because the primary cost of developing multimedia is design and production, the cost per student is reduced as more students use the materials. (3) Technology-based instructional systems can deliver instruction more consistently than can live instructors. (4) With one student per workstation, student privacy can be ensured. (5) Interactive multimedia can ensure mastery. (6) The process of interaction with materials provides increased information retention. (7) With interactive systems, students can explore potentially dangerous subjects without risk. (8) Interactive systems can provide a level of feedback and involvement that is motivating to learners. (9) Greater or more equal access to quality education can be provided through multimedia. (10) Interactive systems allow learners greater control of their own learning processes.

Multimedia Applications

Multimedia materials are either available now or under development in virtually every academic discipline. Thousands of packages are already on the market. The following are a few representative applications of multimedia in college and university teaching.

Science and Mathematics. Multimedia environments allow instructors and students to study concepts that otherwise would be impossible to explore. Students can simulate experiments that would be expensive or dangerous in a laboratory. Instructors can guide learners through microscopic worlds or immense solar systems. For example, in a project at Columbia University, an interactive tutorial teaches dental students the correct angular placement of teeth. This self-paced multimedia system simulates the real placement of teeth and provides remediation and practice as necessary. Preliminary data on student performance indicate considerable improvement with use of this system, when compared to conventional teaching (Norgaard, 1991).

Business. Multimedia can help overcome some of the inadequacies of traditional instructional materials. In business administration, for example, the case study approach often involves reading pages of information about a company. HyperCase, a multimedia project developed at the Massachusetts Institute of Technology, allows students to interact with the case under study. A videodisk containing edited interviews and demonstrations helps learners explore methods for industry research and analysis. These video segments also allow students to review verbal and nonverbal cues that are essential to the decision-making process. Although case study work can be tedious, multimedia can engage and entertain students as well as provide a smooth transition into real-world problems (Davenport and Harber, 1991).

Humanities. Multimedia can bring disciplines together. The Perseus Project at Harvard University involves an interdisciplinary faculty from comparative literature, art history, archaeology, social anthropology, philosophy, political science, religion, and linguistics (Crane, 1991). This project combines CD-ROM and computer technology to provide access to Greek text, English translations, and essays, as well as maps, photographs, drawings, motion video, and color still images of archaeological materials for the study of ancient Greece.

The Shakespeare Project at Stanford University has developed a multimedia package that takes students well beyond the traditional reading and discussion of text. Through a combination of laserdisks and computer software, students see a live performance, study it in detail, interact with the performance, isolate and analyze its components, and simulate its processes (Friedlander, 1988). They can compare film segments of corresponding scenes by different directors of plays such as *Hamlet* and *Macbeth*. Through simulation, students can stage their own interpretations of a play.

The Civil War Interactive is a collaborative project between Kenneth Burns and faculty at George Mason University. Users can access a wide variety of data, charts, photos, audio clips, and graphics related to the Civil War period. Student involvement is aided by context-sensitive coaching (Fontana, 1991).

Multimedia Classrooms

Multimedia materials may be experienced by students in either learning laboratories or independent workstations, or in the more traditional context of a classroom lecture. As multimedia technology has developed, increased attention has been given to the task of modifying the classroom environment to accommodate these systems. Fawson and VanUitert (1990) identified five levels of classrooms that address increasingly sophisticated technological needs. The first two levels, the seminar room and the traditional classroom, contain minimal technology. Level 3, the media-enhanced classroom facility, contains permanently assigned, standard instructional equipment such as an overhead projector and videotape playback system. Level 4, the technology classroom, provides standard media equipment along with a podium-based, multimedia presentation station, including computer, video-data projector, videodisk and CD-ROM players, desktop video camera system, and other resources. Level 5, the technology-enhanced learning environment, adds a local area network of individual workstations. A wide area network, linking the classroom with remote sites on- and off-campus, may also be integrated at this level.

Sophisticated multimedia classrooms have been developed at several colleges and universities. At level 5 on Fawson and VanUitert's scale, the Indiana University-Purdue University at Indianapolis (IUPUI) electronic classroom integrates over fifty audio, video, and computing devices that can be output to three shared projection screens. The options include full-motion video programs, live two-way conferences, high-resolution graphics, data, digital audio and video, and multimedia windows, all under the control of an instructor using a touch-screen computer system.

The planning of a multimedia electronic campus requires cooperation and coordination of many academic and administrative structures. In the case of the IUPUI project, four campus instructional support units—Learning Technologies, Computing Services, University Libraries, and Telecommunications Services—formed a partnership to consider the impact of the technology and to develop and implement a plan. When the project is complete, nearly eighteen hundred multimedia computer workstations will be connected with a campuswide fiber-optic network, permitting access to a wide variety of informational material from media such as videodisk players, satellite-downlink antennas, and CD-ROMs, as well as the full range of computing and library resources. The library will serve as the center for media conversion, management, and switching (Elmore, 1991).

At the University of North Carolina at Chapel Hill (UNC-CH), three types of classrooms have evolved. The goal for each room is to provide a flexible environment for presenting information in a variety of ways, with maximum interaction among the instructor, student, and information (Conway, 1991). The Master Classroom at UNC-CH provides a wide range of media, including two computers connected via Ethernet to a campus cable system for reception and transmission of both video and data. The Computer Classroom is an extension of the Master Classroom concept and includes a microcomputer laboratory. The Teleclassroom allows students and faculty to conduct and participate in live, two-way televised classes located at ten sites across the state. A podium-based presentation unit controls the output of overhead cameras as well as videotapes and slides.

Prerequisites for Integrating Multimedia into Higher Education

The right resources, faculty leadership, and technical support must all be present in order to move a multimedia solution from a desire to a reality (Griffin and Noblitt, 1991). Faculty must match technology with academic goals. It is easy for college committees to focus on the selection, purchase, and installation of software and hardware for multimedia production and delivery, but the primary concern should be the development and integration of multimedia materials into the teaching-learning process.

Faculty Development. The success that multimedia achieves in higher education will be determined mostly by the amount of training and development time available to faculty members. Instructor training often lags behind advances in technology, and the reward systems at many universities do not recognize the instructional development efforts of their faculty. Elmore (1991) observed that in order for faculty to adopt innovative instructional systems such as the electronic classroom at IUPUI, five requirements must be met. The system must be easy to operate by nontechnical users, it must take no more than fifteen minutes to learn, it should be instantly available with little or no preparation, it must be reliable, and it must be powerful.

The design, development, delivery, and evaluation of multimedia courseware is an important concern (Fawson and VanUitert, 1990). Relatively few faculty have sufficient expertise in video production, graphics, authoring, and instructional development to create multimedia projects on their own. Some universities offer workshops to get faculty involved with using multimedia. Others have established technology centers to assist faculty in the development of multimedia projects. For example, the University of Iowa's Second Look Computing Center provides a state-of-the-art multimedia development facility for faculty, administrators, and students interested in developing multimedia materials. The CBEL-Teaching and Learning Technologies Group at Pennsylvania State University also provides instructional design and development assistance, along with resources such as videotapes that showcase successful projects, events that focus on interactive technologies, and publications of interest. The University of Delaware Instructional Technology Center has developed a videotape demonstrating multimedia applications in higher education. In addition, the center offers workshops for faculty on how to use this technology in their classrooms.

Support Services. Unfortunately, institutionwide support services such as those outlined above are rare. While most campuses have media centers or academic computing units to help faculty specify and acquire equipment and software, relatively few provide consultants to help professors conceptualize, plan, and develop multimedia-based instructional materials, or to produce or locate the visuals to be incorporated within them. Many faculty members feel that multimedia is too complex a media form and too time-consuming to prepare to consider taking on development projects on their own. Others have the need and desire but lack the skills or resources to produce effective multimedia materials. It is unlikely that multimedia will have any significant impact on campuses without effective support services for faculty in this area.

Funding. A related problem is lack of funding for equipment, software, and resource materials. Multimedia does not have to be an expensive investment. An instructor can create multimedia by combining existing resources in new ways. Computer software and cabling can link a low-end computer system with a variety of media. In addition, costs can be reduced by networking less-used equipment.

Future of Multimedia

Current discussions between Apple and IBM indicate that multimedia systems will be increasingly compatible. Institutions will be moving from high-cost professional systems to low-cost units that individuals and departments can afford. In addition, easy-to-use authoring systems and an abundance of commercially produced generic information resources will make "repurposing," or revised use of existing materials, easier for faculty.

Trends indicate increasingly easy-to-use, human-computer interfaces. For example, rather than use a keyboard and a mouse, students will manipulate remote controls similar to those used in the new Compact Disk-Interactive (CD-I) systems. A decrease in the physical size of technology is already evident in some of the new notebook-size computers. The computer as we know it will also evolve. Already the computer is transparent in systems such as CD-I. As the physical size of multimedia systems becomes smaller, their sophistication will increase, leading to larger storage capacities and faster access times. Data storage will move away from analog systems and toward high-quality digital storage and delivery systems. Evolving technologies such as holography will be linked with multimedia.

One thing is certain. The list of terminology and acronyms will expand. According to Mohl (1990, p. 123), "We should not put all our eggs in one technological basket. The technological base will continue to change." It is possible that multimedia will one day evolve into what is now defined as virtual reality.

Current trends indicate an exciting future for multimedia. Desktop instructional systems could achieve the same level of market penetration in the 1990s that desktop publishing enjoyed in the 1980s. In fact, with adequate funding and faculty support, computer-based multimedia delivery systems could become the most common form of instructional technology on college campuses by the end of the decade.

References

Barron, A. "Digital Audio in Multimedia Instruction." In D. Dalton and J. Troutner (eds.), *Proceedings of the 33rd Annual International Conference of ADCIS*. Columbus, Ohio: Association for the Development of Computer-Based Instructional Systems, 1991.

Bationo, B. D. "The Effects of Three Forms of Immediate Feedback on Learning Intellectual Skills in a Foreign Language Computer-Based Tutorial." Unpublished doctoral dissertation, Department of Curriculum and Educational Technology, University of Toledo, 1991.

Carlson, P. A. "Square Books and Round Books: Cognitive Implications of Hypertext." *Academic Computing*, 1990, 4 (7), 16–19, 26–31.

Conway, K. L. "Putting Technology in its Place: The Classroom." *IAT Briefings*, 1991, 1 (2), 4–6.

Crane, G. "Hypermedia and the Study of Ancient Culture." *IEEE Computer Graphics and Applications*, 1991, 16, 45–51.

Davenport, G., and Harber, J. D. "Numbers—A Medium That Counts." *IEEE Computer Graphics and Applications,* 1991, *16,* 39–44.

Elmore, G. C. "Planning and Developing a Multimedia Learning Environment." *T.H.E. Journal,* 1991, *18* (7), 83–88.

Fawson, E. C., and VanUitert, D. D. "The Technology Classroom: Alternatives for Future Planning." *TechTrends,* 1990, *35* (4), 28–34.

Fontana, L. A. "The Civil War Interactive." *Instruction Delivery Systems,* 1991, *5* (6), 5–9.

Friedlander, L. "The Shakespeare Project." In S. Ambron and K. Hooper (eds.), *Interactive Multimedia: Visions of Multimedia for Developers, Educators, and Information Providers.* Redmond, Wash.: Microsoft Press, 1988.

Gay, G. K., and Thomas, R. J. "Collaborative Design in a Networked Multimedia Environment." *EDUCOM Review,* Jan.-Feb. 1992, pp. 31–33.

Griffin, S., and Noblitt, J. S. *Multimedia Computing: Getting Started.* Chapel Hill: Institute for Academic Technology, University of North Carolina, 1991.

Jones, L. J., and Smith, S. G. "Can Multimedia Instruction Meet Our Expectations?" *EDUCOM Review,* Jan.-Feb. 1992, pp. 39–43.

Lamb, A., and Myers, D. "Schemes for Organizing Information Exploration Materials in HyperCard: A Taxonomy." *HyperNEXUS: Journal of Hypermedia in Multimedia Studies,* 1990, *1* (1), 10–14.

Miller, R. L. "Learning Benefits of Interactive Technologies." *Videodisc Monitor,* 1990, *8* (2), 14–15.

Mohl, B. "Thoughts on Multimedia Authoring." In J. Baker and R. N. Tucker (eds.), *The Interactive Learning Revolution: Multimedia in Education and Training.* New York: Nichols, 1990.

Nasser, L. D., and McEwen, J. W. "The Impact of Alternative Media Channels: Recall and Involvement with Messages." *AV Communication Review,* 1976, *24* (3), 263–272.

Nicol, A. "Assuming That. . . ." In S. Ambron and K. Hooper (eds.), *Interactive Multimedia: Visions of Multimedia for Developers, Educators, and Information Providers.* Redmond, Wash.: Microsoft Press, 1988.

Norgaard, K. "Dental Students Improve Their Performance." *Instruction Delivery Systems,* 1991, *5* (6), 10–11.

Pea, R. D. "Learning Through Multimedia." *IEEE Computer Graphics and Applications,* July 1991, pp. 58–66.

Strang, H. R. "Pictorial and Verbal Media in Self-Instruction Procedural Skills." *AV Communication Review,* 1973, *21* (2), 225–232.

Tennyson, R. D. "Use of Adaptive Information for Advisement in Learning Concepts and Rules Using Computer-Assisted Instruction." *American Educational Research Journal,* 1981, *18,* 425–438.

ANNETTE C. LAMB is associate professor of curriculum and educational technology at the University of Toledo, Toledo, Ohio.

Academic computing has evolved to encompass a greater number of teaching and learning functions, but further technological change will result in even further institutional and social change.

Academic Computing: How to Address the Teaching and Learning Challenge

Margret Hazen

Computers are becoming an increasingly powerful, versatile, intellectual tool for many professions, and it is not surprising that their use is having a significant effect on teaching and learning in higher education. The nature and extent of that impact is determined by a number of factors, including faculty initiative, staff support, and financial resources. In this chapter, I discuss the impact of the computer on teaching and learning from two perspectives. First, from an academic computing perspective, the historical strands that have led to the current situation are described: and, second, the computer's utility in relation to instructional needs is discussed. I conclude by investigating future trends and strategies for instructional computing in higher education.

Academic and Instructional Computing: Last Thirty Years

Academic computing units have been operational on some campuses for over two decades, providing faculty members with support for their research as well as teaching and learning activities. They are usually but not always distinct from administrative computing units. Within academic computing centers, the instructional support mission has become increasingly important in the last decade.

Early Mainframe Years. The first experiments testing instructional applications of mainframe computers date from the 1950s, with the most vigorous growth in the early to middle 1960s. Engineering and programming courses were the first to adopt the medium, but other disciplines gradually appeared in small numbers. Early applications included business simulations, concordance analyses, statistical analyses, drill and practice modules, and geographical mapping. The most successful applications in terms of endurance and student utilization were statistical applications.

The earliest large-scale, mainframe-based academic computing projects were the pioneering Programmed Logic for Automated Teaching Operation (PLATO), begun at the University of Illinois in 1960, and Time-Shared Interactive Computer-Controlled Television (TICCIT), established by the Mitre Corporation in 1969. Although programs such as these did gain some acceptance, the total number of students, particularly undergraduate students, using computers for learning purposes was small, and usage often focused on research. Experimental projects were as likely to reside within a department as within a computing center, and many were part of a special institute or directed by a committee (Leiblum, 1977). Furthermore, the projects were limited to campuses with direct or time-shared access to mainframe computing resources.

Microcomputing. The 1980s brought dramatic changes in the use of computers by higher education institutions. Beginning with the early and limited use of the TRS-80 and Apple II microcomputers, and spurred by the introduction of the more powerful IBM personal computer and compatibles and the Macintosh, faculty members and students found that the microcomputer offered many advantages over the mainframe and minicomputers. These computers could sit on an individual's desktop and were under that person's control. They offered color, graphics, animation, and audio and were highly interactive. The costs of microcomputers were sufficiently low that they could be acquired by individual faculty members as well as by academic units.

The tremendous jump in power and speed offered by microcomputers, coupled with the corresponding decline in size and cost, led some observers to predict a revolution in education. Between their capacity for interactive and guided learning and their functional diversity—from numbers to text, sound, and graphics—microcomputers had potential applications in almost all academic departments. Since quality software was scarce, faculty members began programming efforts to fulfill these promises. Occasionally, vendor and external funding support provided sophisticated hardware, software, and staff resources, and, by the mid-1980s, software development projects had greatly increased and become an academic computing priority.

Emergence of Information Technology. In the late 1980s, another priority emerged: telecommunications and networked systems. The establishment and improvement of national or wide area networks, such as Bitnet and Internet, along with the development and improvement of local area networks, led to greater functionality and use of networked systems. Simultaneously, libraries increased their rate of automation—online catalogs became increasingly available, as did online data base and citation access. Academic computing units entered into collaborative relationships with campus libraries and offices of telecommunications and, at some institutions, were brought under the same administrative umbrella with them.

By 1990, about two hundred colleges and universities had established chief information officer positions (Penrod, Dolence, and Douglas, 1990). Often reporting directly to the president or chancellor, the chief information officer was given management and advocacy responsibility for academic and administrative computing, data network services, voice (telephone) communications, and other information-related activities.

Reassessment and Refocus of Services. By the end of the 1980s, instructional computing units had emerged as a distinct group within academic computing, and one of their first important tasks was reassessment. Because of a gradual decline in the availability of external funds, instructional software development was found to be too labor-intensive (Child, 1989; Dede, 1989), and emphasis was refocused on questions of access (Hazen and Parker, 1989; Regenstein, 1988). On many campuses, resources were shifted toward development of electronic or master classrooms, equipped with computers and projection systems as well as traditional media equipment and providing an information-rich environment for teaching and learning (Conway, 1990; Watkins, 1991). Both these media-intensive classrooms and corresponding microcomputer laboratories for independent student access benefited from networking. Laboratory managers found that with networking, software disk handling was significantly reduced, upgrades were easier to accomplish, and there was far greater uniformity to the look and feel of individual stations from one location to another.

The present decade opened with economic exigencies and budget cuts at many campuses. A survey conducted by the University of Southern California Center for Scholarly Technology found that 62 percent of the 167 responding public research universities reported cuts in their academic computing budgets for 1991, as did 52 percent of the 181 responding public four-year colleges (Wilson, 1991). As academic computing and instructional support units were expanding their campus roles, resources to fund their activities were shrinking.

As a consequence of increasing functions and declining resources, academic computing units now face a challenging transitional phase. Questions that must be addressed in the coming decade include consideration of which new technologies to adopt, to what extent, and when; which older technologies to discontinue, to what extent, and when; how to support leading edge innovative faculty members while accommodating those new to academic computing; how much, what, and when to decentralize support; how much to shift away from programming and development support to more consultative support; and how much to focus support in specialized disciplinary areas versus general purpose computing.

Impact of Computers on Teaching and Learning

Microcomputers have offered novel opportunities and techniques for instruction ever since experimentation and creativity blossomed in the 1980s. Faculty members, staff, and students saw limitless opportunities for the computer to enhance teaching and learning, but the benefits were not without cost. Present economic conditions have placed a greater emphasis on the value obtained in relation to that cost. Explicit definition of the unique contributions offered by computers over other less costly media has become increasingly important. To become a valuable and viable long-term resource for teaching and learning, the computer must address a unique need in a cost-effective manner. It must be used appropriately and thoughtfully. Software developed by one professor but never used by another, or software used by a professor but once or twice, is not cost-effective. Instead, for long-term impact, it is more desirable for a department or discipline to focus on a powerful and compelling educational problem responsive to technology.

Benefits. The computer can offer benefits to both the learner and the instructor. For the learner, the computer offers an individualized, active learning experience that contrasts sharply with the mostly passive environment of the typical lecture hall. Feedback and evaluation of progress are instantaneous. Since students pace themselves, they can learn at their own rates, which vary across abilities and backgrounds. The computer is patient and permits endless review opportunities. In many instances, especially in the case of simulations, students can have access to experiences that cannot otherwise be brought into the curriculum, whether because of cost, available time, limited space, or danger. Computers can provide visualization of difficult material to help students understand concepts. The opportunities for higher-level learning, multimedia delivery, and learner control often improve students' enthusiasm and motivation for the subject matter and for learning in general.

Because of these and other computer attributes, faculty members are now able to place greater emphasis on concept development and critical thinking experiences. Many are enjoying the role change from instructor-lecturer to facilitator-leader, giving students a more active role in their own learning. Delegation of the routine, the repetition, and the practice to the computer has advantages not only for the learner but also for the professor.

Specific Applications. Computer applications have expanded virtually across the entire college curriculum. Whereas only a small number of research-oriented graduate students used mainframe computers for programming or statistical purposes during the 1960s, undergraduates are now programming in Pascal and using SAS, SPSS, Systat, and Data Desk for data analysis and statistics. Those disciplines that teach mathematical concepts are using applications such as Mathematica, Maple, and Theorist in order to emphasize teaching concepts, while depicting and manipulating highly complex numerical expressions. Business schools rely on spreadsheet applications, and English departments make highly creative use of word-processing software. Computer-driven videodisks are now used by law schools to simulate courtroom conditions, and by chemistry departments to simulate wet laboratories. Psychology students now replicate critical experiments in a computer laboratory, and beginning music composition students create scores that are as easy to revise as term papers produced with word processors. Medical students practice diagnoses with digitized images.

The impact of computers on teaching and learning can be better understood if examined in relation to the needs of a specific discipline. In foreign languages, for example, computers support instruction in two critical areas: helping students master vocabulary and grammar and providing them with realistic and natural language conversation practice, particularly when study abroad is not feasible.

Instructional software that offers students tutorials and practice in foreign language grammar and vocabulary is increasingly available today. As with the language laboratories of the last two decades, the computer laboratory provides opportunities to remove repetitive tasks from the classroom, so that in-class time can be used more productively for spontaneous and creative discussion. Examples of award-winning vocabulary and grammar software (Kozma and Johnston, 1990) include the following: (1) Stephen Clausing's "German Tutor" provides a complete second-year course in German grammar. Students can decide which questions to answer, when to ask for help, and what kind of help, such as an analysis of errors, supplementary explanations, glossary references, or the correct answer. After the lesson, students can request personalized review exercises based on their errors. (2) Frank Dominguez's "Spanish MicroTutor" is a set of thirty modular lessons covering basic Spanish grammar topics for the first three semesters. Each lesson specifies the goals and objectives of that lesson, progresses from general to specific knowledge on the topic, provides exercises and examples to explain the concepts, and identifies the major concepts through visual cues. A dictionary, verb data base, and record-keeping capabilities are also available. (3) Dezso Benedek, Clate Sanders, and Junko Majima's "KanjiMaster" provides students with extensive practice in understanding, pronouncing, and forming Kanji in both simple and compound forms. Students can browse through lists of Kanji words, hear and repeat the sounds, take dictation, practice English-Japanese and Japanese-English equivalents, and watch or practice brush stroke formations and order, a feature not possible in other media.

Two award-winning applications that address the need to simulate natural conversation offer an introduction to applications of the future. Both require a videodisk player in addition to a computer station. Edna Coffin and Amit Schitai's "The Safe Affair—An Interactive Video Hebrew

Lesson" is an interactive video portrayal of a court case in Hebrew. The students serve as the judge while they view both oral and written testimony pertaining to a theft case. They ask questions of witnesses, the defendant, and lawyers. Students select the pace and path of the trial and receive immediate feedback about their comprehension of the trial. Comprehension aids, such as online dictionary and transcriptions in both Hebrew and English, are available to the students, as are information sources such as newspaper articles and interviews with witnesses and lawyers. Gilberte Furstenberg, Janet H. Murray, Stuart Malone, and Ayshe Farman-Farmaian's "À la rencontre de Philippe" is about a student who meets a young man named Philippe, who has been evicted from his girl friend's apartment and needs help in patching up his romance or finding another place to live. Designed to be used at all levels of study, this application offers directed listening tasks as well as the opportunity for advanced students to make and present in class their own minidocumentaries related to the vignette's themes.

Conversation practice applications are just beginning to appear. Most of those currently on the market require relatively complex and more costly equipment. As video is integrated into the desktop computer, these applications will multiply. Vocabulary and grammar practice applications, on the other hand, are beginning to reach a level of sophistication, cost, and ease of use that has been encouraging many to adopt computer language laboratories. Applications do not yet exist for all languages, however, and software is not available for all platforms. Nonetheless, instructional needs are sufficiently strong to motivate continuing development efforts, and computer-based learning packages seem to have an extraordinary future in language training.

Current Trends

The 1980s witnessed the evolution of the computer from a number-crunching tool to an instrument for manipulating text and graphical symbols. The assimilation of full-motion video is one of the most important developments of the 1990s. Analog motion video can now be displayed on the computer desktop, and digital motion video is in the experimental stages. The marriage of video and computing has already had a significant influence on instructional product development and will likely become the dominant form of instructional technology by the middle of the decade.

A second important direction is the growth of electronic networking as a form of distance education. Although distance education today normally refers to one- or two-way transmission of analog video, within the next decade full-motion video may be transported on digital delivery systems. Networking is a growing enterprise, with many proponents at all levels. Envisioned for the future is an "information super-highway" based on optical fiber cable that permits universal access to information. The National Research and Education Network, which has already been funded by Congress, will be able to deliver a multimedia-rich environment to all those connected, many of whom may not have had access before to such a broad range of information.

The extent to which these two, still-evolving technologies—video integration and distance education—become commonplace will be affected significantly by the availability of resources, whether internal or external funding. When resources for experimentation and implementation are limited, as they are likely to be throughout the next decade, then the rates of innovation and adoption diminish. The rate of adoption of the computer as an effective instructional tool from the early stages of the first innovators to the later stages of the succeeding adopters will be affected by resources, as will the pattern of moving from individual adoptions to collaborative and more long-lasting adoptions. Since social change is slower than technological change, this may be an opportunity for social change to catch up with technological change.

Social change of some magnitude has already occurred: computer literacy for the majority of the faculty members and students in higher education. This necessary first step, often word processing, increases the likelihood of the second step, use of the computer for instructional purposes and other applications. While many professionals in academic computing believe that the revolution in instruction anticipated in the early 1980s is still likely to occur, an evolutionary pace is more likely. Within instruction, since resources and incentives have traditionally been inadequate, the norm is typically a failure to adopt innovations. Instead, faculty members have a tendency to build new instructional practices on past practices (Kozma, 1985). As with other instructional technologies, use beyond the experimental and innovation stage is likely to grow more slowly than many expect. After all, Thomas Edison predicted in 1922 that "the motion picture is destined to revolutionize our educational system and that in a few years it will supplant largely, if not entirely, the use of textbooks" (Cuban, 1986, p. 9).

Obstacles

Change requires effort, time, and resources, not only at the individual level but even more so at the organizational level. Fifteen years ago, the obstacles to be overcome before widespread adoption of computers for instruction could occur were costs, attitudes toward computers, and lack of incentives, organizational structure, training and technical support personnel, high-quality materials, and evidence of effectiveness (Seidel, Hunter, Kastner, and Rubin, 1974).

Many of these barriers still exist. For example, while there are indications that the incentive question is being addressed (Boyer, 1990), institutional reward structures still heavily favor research over instructional improvement efforts. Another obstacle, the absence of an appropriate organizational structure and shortage of skilled technical personnel, has been addressed for access to instructional computing materials but not for their development. Only a few academic computing units have qualified personnel available to help faculty create or adapt instructional software and also help them effectively integrate computing into their courses.

However, some improvements are also evident. A major breakthrough has occurred in faculty and student attitudes. Acceptance of computing is far more widespread today than twenty years ago. The computer is no longer a tool to be feared and avoided. It has been particularly well accepted by faculty members and students for word-processing applications. Costs have also improved significantly, so that access is almost universally available through computing laboratories and, on many campuses, multimedia classrooms.

While the call for evidence of effectiveness continues, we have entered a decade in which both faculty members and students possess greater computer literacy and interest than ever before. Further reduction of obstacles will permit even greater use of computers for instructional purposes. Like the blackboard and textbook, the computer is versatile and adaptable and promises to be increasingly reliable, durable, and easy to use—qualities that facilitate adoption (Cuban, 1986).

Strategies for the Future

The task of coping with rapid technological changes, limited funding, and requisite social change presents those in leadership positions with challenging decisions on the future course of academic computing. The need for long-term planning became increasingly obvious throughout the 1980s as newer technologies continued to emerge while the base of users of older technologies broadened. Academic computing units expanded their services accordingly and must now carry out their mission with reduced budgetary resources.

Several strategies are evolving to deal with these planning decisions as flexibly as possible. First, the fostering of self-sufficiency permits support units to trim services for older technologies as they decline in cost and become more familiar and easier to use. This strategy may require the loan or donation of equipment on an extended basis, or it may mean classes, handouts, and newsletters that provide the information necessary to become self-sufficient. Second, decentralization of computing support has become necessary as computing tools are purchased by individuals and are used in different ways in different departments. Many academic computing units now find themselves trying to decide which functions are best centralized and which are best decentralized, with networking and data storage often seen as key central services. Decentralization requires greater sharing of computer facilities and necessitates greater planning and cooperation among intra-university agencies. Early centralization approaches for cost efficiencies are now being reassessed to include decentralization for greater effectiveness.

The third and fourth strategies, and emphasis on flatter organization and collaboration, are interrelated. Flatter organizations not only save money but are also more responsive to change. A flatter organization guided by project management strategies, as well as by line management strategies, is far more flexible. As noted above, not only are technological changes rapid, but they also are leading academic or information technology units beyond their traditional boundaries. Collaborative projects permit the flexibilities of working across traditional unit boundaries without forcing social changes that individuals may not yet be prepared to accommodate. In addition, collaboration offers opportunities for cost sharing.

The future demands flexibility. Technological and social changes will continue. Curriculum revisions and instructional software development will continue to take place. Only the pace of this development remains to be seen. Throughout this evolving situation, faculty roles are much clearer than are staff roles. The organization of the staff support units needed to improve quality, speed, and numbers of uses of computers for teaching and learning has often taken place in an ad hoc fashion, resulting in uneven distribution of instructional computing support across various departments, schools, and divisions.

In the future, there appear to be two possibilities for the positioning of instructional computing. One direction is to continue to organize around the computer as a tool, so that academic computing continues to expand its functions into information technologies and instructional technologies. Basically, instruction would become one of several functions that an information technology unit would address. The library is a model for this type of an approach. The library's products, whether print or nonprint media, and access to these products are provided by one organizational group—the library. Instructional computing hardware and software, and access to these products, can similarly continue to be provided by academic computing or information technology units.

However, higher education is also organized around functions, for example, research, instruction, and administration. Administrative functions have for a long time been organizationally separate from academic functions. Similarly, instructional functions have been separate from research functions. While focusing on instruction, these instructional support units have traditionally utilized a variety of media or technologies. If instructional computing services or functions were positioned within instructional support units, then the computer would become one of several instructional tools alongside a number of other tools or technologies, such as videotapes and printed materials. Graphics, presentation, and desktop publishing tools have already become valuable instructional support assets. As authoring tools and software construction tools continue to improve—to permit development of material without programming skills—instructional support centers may even provide greater software development support.

Organizational change to accommodate technological change is occurring and will continue to evolve. The future for instructional computing within academic computing will involve resolution of some of the tensions between information technology and instructional support units. Both examples currently exist in higher education and create a tension of purpose within these units. Each institution will begin to resolve these issues in its own fashion, based on needs, history, personalities, and campus politics.

One useful first step is self-assessment. Evaluation of the current situation on campus with respect to organizational relationships, responsiveness, and overall effectiveness of academic support service units will help to identify problems that need to be addressed. The next step should be to share the results of changes with other institutions. Progress is more likely when productive strategies are shared. Then, as benefits continue to be articulated and obstacles overcome, we can expect to see instructional computing evolve from its early innovative stages—the isolated, individual projects and changes—to the more firmly established stages of organizational commitment. We are in the early stages of a process that may appear some decades into the future as revolutionary. In the immediate future, however, change will continue in an evolutionary fashion, as social change struggles to keep up with technological change.

References

Boyer, E. L. *Scholarship Reconsidered: Priorities of the Professoriate.* Princeton, N.J.: Carnegie Foundation for the Advancement of Teaching, 1990.

Child, W. C., Jr. "Using Educational Technology Is Labor-Intensive." *EDUTECH Report,* 1990, 5 (5), 1, 6–7.

Conway, K. L. *Master Classrooms: Classroom Design with Technology in Mind.* Institute for Academic Technology, University of North Carolina at Chapel Hill Technology in Higher Education Series, no. 3. McKinney, Tex.: Academic Computing, 1990.

Cuban, L. *Teachers and Machines: The Classroom Use of Technology Since 1920.* New York: Teachers College Press, 1986.

Dede, C. "Planning Guidelines for Emerging Instructional Technologies." *Educational Technology,* 1989, 29 (4), 7–12.

Hazen, M., and Parker, A. "The University of North Carolina at Chapel Hill: Instructional Computing." In W. H. Graves (ed.), *Computing Across the Curriculum: Academic Perspectives.* McKinney, Tex.: Academic Computing, 1989.

Kozma, R. B. "A Grounded Theory of Instructional Innovation in Higher Education." *Journal of Higher Education,* 1985, 56 (3), 300–319.

Kozma, R. B., and Johnston, J. *Catalog of Winners from the 1987–90: EDUCOM NCRIPTAL*

Higher Education Software Awards Competition. Ann Arbor: National Center for Research to Improve Postsecondary Teaching and Learning, University of Michigan, 1990.

Leiblum, M. "Organizational Structuring of CAL Agencies: A Review." *Journal of Computer-Based Instruction,* 1977, *4* (2), 48–53.

Penrod, J. I., Dolence, M. G., and Douglas, J. V. *The Chief Information Officer in Higher Education.* Professional Paper Series, no. 4. Boulder, Colo.: Association for Management of Information Technology in Higher Education, 1990.

Regenstein, C. "After the Honeymoon: Supporting Instructional Microcomputing." Paper presented at the IBM Academic Computing Conference, Indianapolis, Indiana, April 1988.

Seidel, R. J., Hunter, B., Kastner, C., and Rubin, M. "Obstacles to Widespread Use of Computer-Based Curricular Innovations: A Review." *Journal of Computer-Based Instruction,* 1974, *1* (1), 28–31.

Watkins, B. T. "The Electronic Classroom." *Chronicle of Higher Education,* Sept. 4, 1991, pp. A26–A28.

Wilson, D. L. "Many Public Colleges Curb Spending at Campus Computing Facilities." *Chronicle of Higher Education,* Dec. 18, 1991, p. A20.

MARGRET HAZEN, former director of instructional computing at the University of North Carolina at Chapel Hill, is an educational technology consultant in Chapel Hill.

*Computer conferencing offers many opportunities for linking
students and faculty members worldwide. It has proved particularly
effective with women, minorities, and people with disabilities.*

Computer Communications
and Learning

Beryl L. Bellman

Computer electronic messaging (mail, computer bulletin boards, and conferencing) for on-line and distance education has become an accepted
delivery system over the past decade. Electronic mail is essentially a one-
to-one or one-to-many form of communication. The writer of the message
sends it to another user either by leaving it on the same mainframe or host
computer, called a *server,* or by sending it on to another server at a distant
location. In academia, Bitnet (Because It's Time Network) is a version of
this method, whereby mail is sent to a distribution computer, which then
forwards the mail to a mainframe where the receiver has an account. This
procedure is referred to as *store and forward* as opposed to a procedure in
which sender and receiver access the same machine. Some users of electronic mail send to distribution lists and thereby are able to send the same
message simultaneously to a group of receivers.

  In contrast to electronic mail, computer bulletin boards and conferencing
are methods for sending files from a sender to a file on a mainframe that is
shared by others at various locations. All users must access the same mainframe, either by direct dial or by using a public data communications network.
The difference between a bulletin board and conferencing is that the latter
uses a much more sophisticated type of software, permitting users to search,
branch comments into topics and replies, vote, and use a number of other
functions. The two methods are similar in that users post information that is
later read in sequence by other users accessing the board or conference.
Because of the advantages of conferences, participants are able to sustain long
interactions, whereas most bulletin board discussions are more limited in
length and tend to involve fewer interactants.

These technologies are useful in a variety of ways, ranging from methods to augment and supplement regular coursework to distance education applications. Computer conferencing and electronic mail can be used to provide writing-across-the-curriculum experiences and also to teach essential computer concepts as a integral part of every course. Students engage each other and the faculty in discussion group conferences, which improve critical thinking and promote learning. When used in distance education, conferencing lessens the distance and alienation of the student from the professor and other students in the course. In this chapter, I discuss some of these advantages in the context of an academic computer network used for on-line education in the United States, Canada, Latin America, Europe, and, soon, Africa.

There are now educational host conferencing systems at universities in the United States, Canada, Britain, Ireland, France, Germany, Sweden, Japan, and, to a limited extent, Russia. Students either log on to a host computer at their own university or else access a data packet switching network.[1] Students read or download all waiting items in one or more computer conferences for the class. They then respond by writing their comments on what was read, very often after having taken time to reflect and do research on their electronic class contributions. These mediated or "virtual" classrooms differ from face-to-face classes in that students are required to be much more active and to interact not only with the faculty member teaching the class but also with the other students enrolled. In this way, on-line education is less competitive than traditional methods and is more of a collaborative learning experience (Hiltz, 1984).[2]

A Brief History of Computer Conferencing in Higher Education

According to Feenberg (1988), the first course taught through computer conferencing was an English course at Colorado College in 1981. In that same year, the Western Behavioral Sciences Institute established an executive training program, the School of Management and Strategic Studies, that conducts advanced seminars using computer conferencing. Distinguished faculty from major international universities conduct seminars for senior-level executives, who participate from around the world. In 1984, Starr Roxanne Hiltz evaluated the effectiveness of computer conferencing by introducing courses in engineering and sociology into the curriculum of the New Jersey Institute of Technology (NJIT). These courses were the first of their kind to be offered for credit and grades. As a result of that project, Hiltz and Murray Turoff, the developer of the Electronic Information Exchange System computer conferencing system at NJIT, and his colleagues published a series of monographs and essays demonstrating the effectiveness of the technology, both for the delivery of educational programs and for decision making in electronic meetings conducted in corporate and academic settings (Hiltz, 1984; Hiltz and Turoff, 1978; Kerr and Hiltz, 1982).

In 1985, Paul Levinson and Tina Vozick of the New School for Social Research in New York, in cooperation with university extension, developed the program Connected Education. This was the first degree program that solely used computer conferencing and messaging, without any other means of interaction (Levinson, 1988). Connected Education now offers both a bachelor's and a master's degree in media studies.

Within the past few years, a number of institutions have introduced computer conferencing as a regular method to augment existing lectures. In 1984, the University of Guelph, in Ontario, Canada, developed its own conferencing system to use in seminars in the School of Extension Education. Since that time, faculty and staff have extensively developed their own conferencing software and introduced it to a number of other universities in the United States and Europe. Also, the Ontario Institute for Studies in Education has established a program in which students take graduate-level seminars in virtual and actual settings. In some of the latter, students are asked to engage in both face-to-face and on-line projects in groups of various sizes (Zimmerer, 1988; Harasim, 1986).

Conferencing has also been used extensively at the University of Arizona for electronic meetings in both university departments and research institutes, as well for instruction in several departments, including Spanish, English, and education (Caldwell, Van Nest, Tynan, and Leach, 1987). Also, for several years the Maricopa Community College Office of Instructional Technologies in Phoenix has been offering courses in English composition and other subject areas by computer conferencing. The New York Institute of Technology Open University (Zimmerer, 1988) and the British Open University (Kaye, 1987) have also used computer conferencing to supplement existing media programs.[3]

The BESTNET Experiment

In 1985, a group of colleagues and I drew upon several of these experiments to create the Binational English and Spanish Telecommunications Network (BESTNET). At that time, we used computer conferencing and electronic mail as an interactive component to bilingual video lectures or telecourses. We were initially concerned with how to improve student feedback to instructional television courses that were microwaved to a satellite campus of San Diego State University, about 125 miles away, adjacent to the Mexican border. Students were greatly dissatisfied with the video courses, often feeling like second-class students compared to those taking the same course on the main campus.

The university attempted to provide student feedback by allowing students to telephone the instructor during class to ask questions. However, only a few students took advantage of this procedure, and the majority of students continued to feel alienated. We also determined that questions asked in lecture classes were most often more relevant to course management than to content. We introduced computer conferencing as a method for holding student discussion groups and laboratory sessions, and electronic mail as a method for the faculty member to answer students' questions during on-line office hours. In this manner, all students were required to interact with the professor and with each other about the content of the lectures and text.

Our project originally involved the production of a series of Spanish language-English translation distance education video courses in the sciences, mathematics, and computer and information fields. The courses were made interactive through use of computer conferencing. In our evaluation of the project, we learned that students were particularly responsive to the computer conferencing interactions and did not need as much formal presentation of lecture materials by video as we had originally believed. As a result, we began to rely more heavily on computer conferencing interactions for both the presentation and discussion of materials, and to use video and other materials to supplement or present information for those discussions. Because we found conferencing to be so effective as the dominant or stand-alone form of course delivery, we then explored applications of computer conferencing in different kinds of courses.

We are now involved with three kinds of courses delivered through computer communications. In the first format, students do not see the instructor but communicate with him or her in computer conferences or virtual classrooms, during synchronous on-line office hours utilizing the computer phone or chat utility, and with private electronic mail messages. In the second format, faculty make formal video lecture presentations to complement the discussions in computer conferences. In the third format, faculty members conduct part of the course on line and also have face-to-face interaction with the classes. These courses are team-taught among several institutions. Students participate on line with faculty and students at other campuses, with the elected option of a local faculty member offering a section of the course on his or her own campus.

Evaluating Student Outcomes

The Virtual Classroom studies of Hiltz and Turoff (Hiltz, 1984; Kerr and Hiltz, 1982; Hiltz and Turoff, 1978), our BESTNET studies (Arias and Bellman, 1987), and studies on educational conferencing in Europe (Kaye, 1987; Adrianson, 1985; Adrianson and Hjelmquist, 1985) report no significant differences in performance between students taught in face-to-face and students taught via computer conferencing, which supports the viability of conferencing for distance learning programs. These studies also found that computer conferencing worked particularly well in minority student education, a consequence of the self-paced timing of instruction, the ability of students to receive immediate feedback about their errors, and the ability to ask questions in an anonymous communicative setting.

Hiltz and Turoff (1978) described how computer conferencing is especially viable for people with disabilities. In addition to the obvious benefit of interacting from more available and manageable physical environments, the students do not suffer from prejudices experienced in regular classrooms. Students are evaluated solely on the basis of their academic performance. All physical handicaps are invisible to the medium, and students are treated as full members of the class without having to experience discrimination because of physical appearance, speech impairments, or other factors that often inhibit their participation in face-to-face classroom situations.

The same group of studies also demonstrated that female students do very well with the medium. In face-to-face interactions, women are often forced into a facilitation role and many times lose turns to speak in conversation with men because of implicit sexism in interactions. In computer-mediated discourse, women are able to express themselves much more easily and fully without being interrupted or ignored.

This ability of the medium to encourage more assertive involvement in the education process among traditionally apprehensive and passive learners was demonstrated in a BESTNET course taught at a rural satellite campus of San Diego State University, situated in a community on the U.S.-Mexico border and serving mostly adult Hispanic students. The faculty member wanted to determine if the use of anonymous pen names for students in the conferences would elicit more candid comments about the poems and essays required in his course on modern American literature. He conducted the course via a host computer at the Western Behavioral Sciences Institute, which provided both topics and reply branches in the conferences.

Each student was assigned a topic with its own reply string. In this way, students commented on the class assignments and also on what each other had written. The class elicited several hundred comments, which ranged from detailed commentaries on the assigned texts to debates among the students over the interpretations. One of the male students was particularly outspoken about the homosexual references of several of the authors. The majority of those in the class were adult Hispanic women, who, in the context of the anonymity provided both through the medium and their pen names, engaged him in heated debate. By the end of the course, several of the women students had become very assertive and had no inhibitions against openly debating his ideas.

In the evaluation of the experiment, the faculty member strongly maintained that the development of such assertiveness by the women in the course could not have occurred in the face-to-face classroom setting. The computer conference was used as a supplement to face-to-face lectures and class discussions. When the students met in class, they did not engage in heated debate, nor was any attempt made to criticize the ideas and comments of anyone in the class. Although the class began with no one knowing anyone else's identity, the students soon began to share their pen names with friends. Within the first two weeks, either through direct revelation or second-hand gossip, all identities became known. Consequently, the use of anonymous identities was a valuable pedagogical resource for initiating the discussion, but it was the anonymity provided by the medium that sustained it and promoted the strong assertive remarks.

Providing Access to New Learning Environments

In the study *Ivory Towers, Silicon Basements* (Fund for the Improvement of Post-Secondary Education, 1988), three recommendations were made in regard to equity for nontraditional learners: (1) Careful consideration of issues related to equity should be part of any plan for introducing computing into the curriculum. (2) Access to computing means recognition that different students have different needs and that some programs should be tailored accordingly. And (3) programs that enable students to overcome isolation and passivity in their learning experiences will do the most to promote equal educational opportunities and experiences. The BESTNET project addresses each of these recommendations in providing new interactive technologies to nontraditional and minority learners. The project is unique in its tailoring of both program and software to meet their particular needs and requirements. By fostering electronic discussions both within course conferences and in tutorials and by employing study groups and electronic office hours, the project helps students overcome the isolation and passivity that hinders academic performance.

Research Findings

The BESTNET project now involves hundreds of students each year from over a dozen institutions in the United States and Mexico. The following findings were the products of research conducted by BESTNET faculty, using a combination of user interviews and content analyses of conferences for various types of courses and collaborative research projects.

1. The technology greatly augments regular classroom instruction and is a viable technology for off-campus or distance education.

2. Computer conferencing is a viable interactive component of video or instructional television courses because it provides individualized attention to student needs and requirements that cannot be obtained through traditional methods of audio and video feedback.

3. Computer conferencing supports a Socratic method of instruction, whereby students are actively involved participants in the learning process rather than passive recipients, and the anonymity of the technology promotes discussion that otherwise would be inhibited out of concern for negative face-to-face feedback from other students.

4. Computer conferencing promotes participation and learning in traditionally apprehensive students. In traditional classroom situations, many students are often reluctant to interact with anyone other than their instructors, whereas computer communications promotes student-to-student interaction. The technology is particularly useful for facilitating group discussion and criticism in virtually all areas of the curriculum.

5. The technology facilitates writing across the curriculum and greatly improves editorial and logical skills. It is particularly viable for reaching linguistically and culturally diverse learners.

6. Computer-naive students learn with a facility equal to that of students who are more sophisticated with the technology. Social science and humanities students with no more than basic word-processing skills learned and accepted the technology at an equivalent level with students taking advanced computer science courses.

7. Computer communications tend to improve literacy even when a liberal attitude is taken toward grammar, syntax, and spelling. Writing skills improve with active participation in computer conferences.

8. The medium promotes more critical than hostile competitive discussion.

Globalizing the Network

Recently, BESTNET was extended to include students and colleagues at several sites in Latin America and Canada, and it will soon be involving universities in Kenya and Zimbabwe. This extension was accomplished by developing our distributed computer conferencing and videotext network over Internet/NSF-NET, which interconnects over three-hundred thousand host computers at university campuses in the United States, Canada, Europe, and Asia. At the present time, there are no Internet nodes in sub-Saharan Africa, and only a few in Latin America. However, to implement the project immediately, the network was developed by utilizing public or government-owned data networks currently operating in Africa and Latin America. These networks permit the networking of computers in select countries in both Africa and Latin America, which then transmit to the California State University System and computer communications network (CSU-NET), which operates a public data network gateway into its system. CSU-NET is the largest internal academic regional network in the United States. Once connected to it, international users are able to access a variety of data bases and other services available both in BESTNET and elsewhere on Internet, including the National Science Foundation supercomputer network.

In Latin America, we are developing a graduate degree program in nursing and health sciences in conjunction with the California State University System nursing program. The Latin American program, managed by the International Health Manpower Project, provides video-based materials to select Latin American countries and then conducts seminars using computer conferencing discussions. In Africa, we are initiating collaboratively taught courses between faculty at institutions in the United States and the Department of Journalism and Communications at the University of Nairobi in Kenya, and new technology courses with colleagues at the University of Zimbabwe.

Our project uses a fully distributed computer communications network. Rather than logging on to a computer in the West, international users operate their own mainframes that are internationally interconnected or distributed. In this manner, the project achieves the effective transfer of the technology to those countries and the building of local capacity in them. We believe that BESTNET will greatly facilitate the use of computer communications, both for scientific research and for distance education programs involving colleges and universities around the world. This project is, of course, not the only educational network in existence. However, it is an exemplary model for presenting these new technologies.

Notes

1. In the United States and Europe, the most commonly used data packet network is Internet, which was initially set up by the Department of Defense but in the early 1970s was transformed into an educational and scientific network.
2. Hiltz (1984) refers to computer conferencing courses as "virtual classrooms." I use the term *mediated classrooms* because, in addition to conferencing, many of the courses to which I refer integrate other media, such as video, audio, videotext, and other data base services.
3. Many organizations are beginning to use computer conferencing and electronic mail to establish working groups for all stages of product development and marketing, as well as for customer support. Several international companies even operate their own communications satellite networks in order to interconnect employees from all of the countries in which they are involved. In this manner, employees collectively develop projects, without having any knowledge of the personal identities of their coworkers, who are geographically dispersed around the country and the world.

References

Adrianson, L. *Group Communication Via Computer: Social Psychological Aspects of the Com System*. Göteborg, Sweden: Department of Psychology, University of Göteborg, 1985.
Adrianson, L., and Hjelmquist, E. *Small Group Communication in Two Media: Face-to-Face Communication and Computer-Mediated Communication*. Göteborg, Sweden: Department of Psychology, University of Göteborg, 1985.

Arias, A., and Bellman B. "BESTNET: International Cooperation Through Interactive Spanish/English Translation Telecourses." *Technology and Learning,* 1987, *1* (3), 3-5.

Caldwell, R., Van Nest, W., Tynan, A., and Leach, R. "Conferencing Selection and Implementation: University of Arizona Case History." Paper presented at the Second Symposium on Computer Conferencing and Allied Technologies, University of Guelph, Canada, August 1987.

Feenberg, A. "The Planetary Classroom." In E. Stefferud, O. J. Jacobsen, and P. Schicker (eds.), *Message Handling Systems and Distributed Applications.* The Hague: North Holland Press, 1988.

Fund for the Improvement of Post-Secondary Education (FIPSE) Technology Study Group. *Ivory Towers, Silicon Basements: Learner-Centered Computing in Postsecondary Education.* Washington, D.C.: EDUCOM, 1988.

Harasim, L. "Computer Learning Networks: Educational Applications of Computer Conferencing." *Journal of Distance Education,* 1986, *1* (1), 59-70.

Hiltz, S. R. *Online Communities: A Case Study of the Office of the Future.* Norwood, N.J.: Ablex, 1984.

Hiltz, S. R., and Turoff, M. *The Network Nation: Human Communication Via Computer.* Reading, Mass.: Addison-Wesley, 1978.

Kaye, T. "Introducing Computer-Mediated Communication into a Distance Education System." *Canadian Journal of Educational Communications,* 1987, *16* (2), 156-166.

Kerr, E., and Hiltz, S. R. *Computer-Mediated Communication Systems: Status and Evaluation.* New York: Academic Press, 1982.

Levinson, P. *Mind at Large: Knowing in the Technological Age.* Greenwich, Conn.: JAI Press, 1988.

Zimmerer, J. "Computer Conferencing: A Medium for Facilitating Interaction in Distance Education." In D. Ely (ed.), *Educational Media and Technology Yearbook.* No. 14. Englewood, Colo.: Libraries Unlimited, 1988.

BERYL L. BELLMAN is associate professor in Communication Studies, California State University, Los Angeles. He has conducted extensive cross-cultural and intercultural communications research in Africa and Latin America.

Distance education applications continue to grow, fueled by pressing needs, increased technological capabilities, lean budgets, and new partnerships.

Distance Education: Meeting Diverse Learners' Needs in a Changing World

Marcia A. Baird, Mavis K. Monson

Distance education offers tremendous opportunities, as well as challenges, to today's educators. The demand for flexible, relevant educational programs is high. The technological alternatives and capabilities for linking teachers and learners are increasing. At the same time, tight financial conditions confront many higher education institutions. In response to these opportunities and challenges, distance education is advancing, taking on added importance for many institutions, and influencing traditional education in a "convergence" of educational practices (Smith and Kelly, 1987).

Simply stated, distance education occurs when the instructor and students are physically distant from one another (Keegan, 1986; Verduin and Clark, 1991). Other key elements of distance education—as opposed to distance learning—are the influence of an educational organization, the use of educational media such as print, and two-way communication between student and teacher or facilitator of learning.

Time, in addition to distance, is a factor. Educators no longer employ distance education simply to extend traditional courses to geographically isolated students and adults. Today adults from urban as well as rural communities enroll in distance education courses, participating from college classrooms, corporate offices, and homes. More than distance, it is increasingly the time demands and constraints of today's adults that shape many programs. Using desktop and home computers, they have quickly become accustomed to accessing large amounts of data almost instantaneously. This expectation of quick access, combined with today's busy lifestyles, means that learners will increasingly want and need education and training on demand.

Evolution of Distance Education Technology

Distance education traces its roots to four primary media: print, voice, video, and computer (Charles, 1991). Today, distance education runs the spectrum from correspondence courses to radio, audiocassettes, and audio-conferencing, and from educational television to computer-based multimedia courses.

Correspondence study dates to the mid-1800s and remained the mainstay of distance education throughout the first half of the twentieth century. Use of radio began in the 1920s, on a one-way basis, bringing classes to rural and remote areas. In contrast, although the telephone became commonplace in homes and businesses during that time, it was not until the 1950s and 1960s that its use in distance education, with amplified telephones and bridges to link calls, became feasible.

Television as a medium for course delivery began in the 1960s, coming into full flower in the following decades. Early programming involved one-way broadcasting, using the infrastructure of public television and commercial stations. After many years of one-way broadcasting, the change to more interactive modes became more common in the late 1970s and 1980s, with user data indicating that effective course design must include more than "talking heads."

Computer technology has dramatically enlarged the range of tools available for distance education programming. It is also increasingly shifting distance education from classroom settings to individual offices and homes. Computer conferencing (linking individuals at a distance with modems and personal computers for meetings or education) has grown dramatically in the last several years. Indeed, today's desktop computers have as much computing power as large mainframes had just ten years ago.

One emerging computer-based technology that shows great potential for distance education is the personal computer with hypertext and hypermedia software. Through its linking power, users can access a wide variety of resources residing on the computer's hard drive, in external devices such as videodisk storage, and in remote information data bases (through a modem). Hypermedia provides access not only to print and graphics but also to sound and video in combinations that allow the user to see (or hear) the information in the form desired. These applications, as well as the continuing work at the Massachusetts Institute of Technology Media Laboratory on holographic imaging and virtual reality (Brand, 1987), will certainly play a role in the distance education technologies of the future.

Distance Teaching Universities

Some institutions were founded specifically to develop and teach distance education courses. Two examples are the British Open University (OU) and the University of Mid-America (UMA). OU, founded in 1969, offers more than 250 courses to 130,000 students each year. It is recognized internationally as a pioneering distance education institution, successfully using a course team approach and incorporating print, radio, television, audiocassettes, and tutorial learning into its programs.

In contrast, UMA was dissolved in 1982, just eight years after its start. A consortium of eleven midwestern universities, UMA was founded as a media-based distance education institution. Television, radio, telephone, audiocassettes, and newspapers were used to deliver instruction. Zigerell (1991) concludes that UMA failed because its courses did not meet broad student needs and its elaborate television productions forced a strong dependence on outside funding.

Higher Education's Role in Distance Education

Historically, higher education has pioneered many distance education efforts. For example, telecommunications is at the heart of a new distance education system offered by the University of Maine System. Under the leadership of the University of Maine at Augusta, the state is using a combination fiber-optic and microwave network to build the Community College of Maine, a community college system without walls.

These facts spurred the initiative: two-thirds of the state's population lives beyond a reasonable commuting distance from any of the seven university campuses; in 1985, Maine ranked last among the states in adults participating in higher education and nearly that low in the percentage of high school graduates who continued their education.

The seven University of Maine campuses are equipped with two-way, full-motion video. Point-to-point microwave and Instructional Television Fixed Service (ITFS) extend interactive television programs—university and high school courses, legislative hearings, and training seminars and meetings—to more than seventy remote sites. Now, 85 percent of the state's population is within fifteen minutes of a remote "campus."

The University of Wisconsin-Extension, working with and through the twenty-six University of Wisconsin (UW) campuses, uses a mix of distance education systems to reach adult learners throughout the state, across the country, and internationally. It enrolls more than 11,500 students annually in independent study (correspondence) courses; it also reaches more than 35,000 adults annually using a variety of distance education technologies, including ITFS, statewide radio and television, and teleconferencing.

More than a quarter-century ago, UW established a private line audio network. Its original purpose was to deliver continuing education programs to Wisconsin physicians. Today, the network delivers diversified programs; more than fifty different UW departments use Extension's Educational Teleconference Network to reach participants at 170 statewide locations.

Responding to current needs of students and professionals, the UW recently implemented a new software-based audiographics system. The system builds on the UW's experiences with freeze-frame video and a telewriter system, dating back to 1968. Today, the WisView audiographics system links students at more than two dozen UW campuses. In addition, the network extends to in-plant sites on a course-by-course basis to reach professionals at General Motors, IBM, AT&T, Honeywell, and smaller companies and agencies.

Credit and noncredit courses are offered in such areas as technical Japanese, engineering project management, concrete foundation design, and reading German. Students view course graphics, images, and text on a twenty-inch computer monitor; they use an audio link and visuals tools, including a graphics tablet and scanner, to interact with the instructor and fellow participants.

Growth has also occurred in videoconferencing. Seventy county UW-Extension offices and sixteen UW campuses have satellite downlinks, pulling down programming from UW departments and nationwide providers.

Why Systems Are Successful

How does an institution define a "successful" distance education program? The criteria are different across institutions. For some, success is found in the number of enrollments, courses, or remote sites. For others, it is use of the latest technology, faculty acceptance, cost-effectiveness, years of operation, or a combination of all of these factors.

The success of UW-Extension with distance education can be traced to several characteristics:

Compatible with Mission. UW-Extension, as part of a land grant institution, has always had a strong outreach mission. Many of its faculty use various technologies to extend classrooms to the outer edges of Wisconsin and beyond. This outreach philosophy spurs many faculty to be more open than are some resident faculty to new ways of extending and improving education.

Meeting Learners' Needs for Content and Credentials. Another key success factor is the process used to decide which courses to teach. Courses must meet the needs of the learners in content and, if necessary, credentials. Depending on the clientele group, the course focus may be narrow or broad-based. For example, actively employed professionals generally seek courses with a narrow content focus in order to acquire specific information that builds on existing knowledge or to solve work-related challenges. Conversely, nontraditional adult students who seek a degree generally want broader-based courses to provide credit toward lower-division requirements. Zigerell (1991, p. 50) notes, in this case, that the curriculum policy, if not carefully planned, creates "little more than a grab bag of discrete courses rather than a curriculum."

In Wisconsin, the need for curriculum planning for the adult professional is considered essential. The increasingly self-supporting nature of departmental budgets demands the assessment of student needs before promotional dollars are spent on courses. Advisory (curriculum planning) committees are considered essential to program planners. Committee members, including educators and representatives from the potential clientele group, often meet on the statewide network to allow broad input.

Emphasis on Faculty Training. Distance education introduces some of the same challenges of face-to-face teaching, but it also adds new ones. Successful distance education systems not only orient faculty to a particular delivery technology but also help them capitalize on its strengths. Hands-on workshops, for example, allow new UW teleconference instructors to experience what it is like to be a distant learner. *Bridging the Distance* (Monson, 1978) and other UW-Extension publications offer faculty tips on how to encourage participation from distant students, how to design visuals, and how to break down geographical barriers.

Emphasis on Site Support. Successful institutions also focus on the importance of the distance education learning site and of on-site support. Learners cannot learn if training rooms are locked, if equipment is not set up, and if connections to remote teachers are not made. Students, as well as faculty, need instruction not only on how to operate the technology but also on how to effectively learn at a distance.

Trends in Distance Education

To evaluate the state of distance education today, educators must consider current trends in the field.

Pressing Learner Demands and Needs. Adult learning is the largest and most rapidly growing education sector in the nation. Distance education programs can respond effectively to the requirements of an increasingly trained work force and to the ways that people live and work today. Training and retraining opportunities must be delivered at convenient times and places, particularly as adults try to add part-time continuing education and credit courses to lives that are already juggling full-time job and family responsibilities.

Distance education is not only recasting the traditional campus but also reshaping corporate education and training. Fueling this trend are business and industry's need to keep pace with rapid technological developments, increasing global competition, and a reduced work force. There are now more than two hundred satellite networks, for example, devoted to corporate education and training, offering specialized programming to such organizations as computer companies, automobile dealers, financial firms, and pizza chains. A recent conversation with a downlink coordinator at a major corporation revealed that this site alone was downlinking fifteen noncredit programs (each three to six hours long) and sixty credit programs (each one hour long) via satellite every business day.

Educational Reform and Coordination. Many educators and state policymakers are looking at distance education as one way to extend and improve education. In a canvass of the fifty states, Hezel (1992) found that nearly all states are planning or implementing telecommunications systems for education. Part of the overhauling of many educational systems involves increased funding for all education programs, including distance delivery systems.

As states deal with lean budgets, growing agency requests, and increasingly complex telecommunications alternatives, many now require all state educational agencies, as well as other state agencies, to cooperatively plan distance education systems. Some states and institutions have begun to structure themselves around technology and distance education. Oregon, for example, recently established the new state agency Ed-Net to provide educational telecommunications.

At the same time, demands for educational reform are coming from other sectors of society. The United States Distance Learning Association (1991), representing universities, K–12 schools, and corporate training interests, recently presented a set of education and communications policy recommendations for federal, state, and local governments at a congressional briefing. USDLA recommends the development of new education, communication, and information policies and regulations so that the nation can benefit from the powerful new distance learning tools.

New Partnerships. Distance education is forging new relationships among education institutions as well as between education and business. Fueling this cooperation are state mandates and shrinking educational dollars, as well as aggressive initiatives by telecommunications service and equipment vendors to position themselves as educational partners.

Within states, there are growing district, regional, and statewide consortia. Multistate systems are also helping education institutions pool program planning, production, and marketing resources. The National Technological University (NTU) currently draws its faculty from forty engineering schools at major universities. Through satellite delivery, NTU offers entire degree programs and continuing education courses to technical professionals and managers at 350 sites nationwide. More than thirty higher education institutions have joined AG*SAT, a service that originates, distributes, and shares residential and extension programming via satellite.

Increased Technology Options and Integration. Some distance education delivery systems remain singular in focus. Many correspondence courses, for example, continue to be entirely print-based. Other distance education courses combine several formats, such as educational television programs linked with a strong print component. Increasingly, integrated distance education systems, combining audio, video, and graphics components, are becoming a driving force behind new distance education applications.

Impact on Traditional Education. Distance education systems are changing the way that educators teach and the way that adults learn and access education. As a result, distance education is impacting traditional education. Smith (1987, p. 32) states that educators teaching at a distance have been forced to consider alternative teaching methods and, as a consequence, have had to optimize the use of such tools as print, graphics, and audiocassettes. He concludes that distance education has also influenced the development of course materials used in higher education, offering the opportunity of cumulative improvement in the quality of teaching. Many educators who have taught at a distance, for example, remark on how their experience has forced them to better organize their content, prepare better print resources, and pay more attention to interaction with learners.

Distance education formats are also increasingly being integrated into face-to-face instruction to enrich and improve courses. Mixed media courses, for example, often supplement traditional lectures with computer simulations, videoconferences, and electronic mail components.

Increased Visibility. Charles Wedemeyer, a noted University of Wisconsin educator, spent many years promoting distance education to U.S. higher education institutions. The title of this book, *Learning at the Back Door* (Wedemeyer, 1981), acknowledges the field's second-class status at the time. A decade later, distance education has made considerable advances; it is no longer the exclusive domain of a few universities. Distance education articles in the *Wall Street Journal* and *Business Week,* the formation of distance education associations and conferences, the recent national movement to explore the launching of an educational satellite, and the dissemination of publications such as the *American Journal of Distance Education* reflect only a few examples of increased interest and activity by both education and business. In response to the growing interest and needs within the field, the University of Wisconsin at Madison is also developing a noncredit certificate of professional development in distance education—to be delivered in distance education formats.

Implications for Educators

Many forces are converging to advance distance education, including increased needs, improved technologies, and falling prices of the technologies. Whatever the guiding forces, however, faculty still need to respond in several areas to meet learners' needs.

Need for a Discipline of Distance Education. In 1992, almost 150 years after the first distance education course, the field is still struggling to develop as a discipline. For example, it was not until a decade ago that the

International Council on Correspondence Education deleted "correspondence" from its name and changed it to "distance," recognizing the changed focus of its membership. Moore (1973) noted that to progress, distance education needed to describe and define itself, and to begin building a theoretical framework. Holmberg (1989) and Keegan (1986) reinforced the need for testable hypotheses.

Literature exists that explores the effectiveness of print, radio, teleconferencing, and other media used in distance education, but it is scattered, tends toward case study reporting, and generally has no theoretical base. This lack of an organized body of research hinders not only the credibility of the field but also its ability to attract new faculty. With the tenure process a reality, and without a theoretical base on which to build, it is difficult to pursue scholarly work and publish findings. Distance educators tend to come from established faculty who have already achieved tenure, or from the ranks of other professors who teach on an adjunct basis.

There are practical concerns as well that stem from the lack of a data base of information. Without this base to provide the "theory-into-practice" guidelines so needed in distance education, the day-to-day teaching process tends to reinvent the wheel with each endeavor.

Greater Faculty Involvement. For most faculty, teaching is, and should be, the first priority. Increasingly, however, distance education systems thrust faculty directly into new areas of the educational process. For example, an understanding of how to design effective graphics for teleconferencing, manage audio interaction, organize computer graphics files, and budget for course delivery at a distance may seem far removed from teaching. But these are some of the tasks faced by distance education instructors today.

Faculty need to deepen their understanding of distance education, regardless of a particular delivery system. At the same time, they need to understand the unique values and features of chosen delivery systems so that they can apply these new education tools effectively and understand their risks. Technical problems of new systems, for example, can frustrate faculty who are accustomed to being in total control of classroom teaching.

Improved Course Design. The ultimate payoff for the expanding capacity of distance education systems may be new applications and improved course designs. Some faculty readily admit that the courses designed to take advantage of new distance education systems are, in fact, often superior to their traditional classroom presentations.

Learning at a distance is not easy. Today's distance education courses, using technologies ranging from response keypads to interactive, multimedia software, offer higher levels of student interactivity than ever before available. If faculty can use these tools to build more exciting and effective courses, then adults will be increasingly motivated to enroll and reenroll in distance education courses.

Program Planning. Currently, educators have more tools than ever before to deliver programs at a distance. Clearly, the capacity will only grow. Several companies, for example, are introducing technology that will significantly increase the number of television channels per satellite transponder. Instead of programming one or two channels per transponder, new developments will allow providers to transmit twelve or more channels per transponder. At the same time, more public and private organizations will be looking for high-quality distance education programming. The question is whether educators will be ready to take advantage of this expanding capability and audience. Many faculty are just now starting to explore distance education. The tasks of exploring, planning, and creating new courses (or adapting existing courses) for new delivery systems usually take a year or more.

Increased Staff Support. Technology is moving fast on many fronts. What these technologies add in increased access and opportunities for distance education, they also add in increased support needs of faculty and students.

As the technology of distance education becomes more diverse, increasingly sophisticated support organizations will be needed to manage distance education networks and help faculty design, produce, and deliver courses. In addition, staff will need to track applications, assess emerging technologies, and plan for growth.

As digital and analog technologies continue to merge, distance education applications, among others, will also require increasing interdependence between what may still be discrete campus units: broadcasting, teleconferencing, video production, and computer technology. Mergers may occur at some institutions.

Finally, distance education course delivery will challenge many other institutional support units, such as student registration and records, libraries, printing departments, bookstores, and computer services, to be responsive to the needs of off-campus learners.

Need for Faculty Training. Most higher education faculty receive limited training in how to improve their teaching methods. Faculty in distance education programs are no different. Gehlauf, Shatz, and Frye (1991) found that interactive television course instructors believe that training is important and want more hands-on training, a need earlier identified by Carl (1986). In seven case studies by the U.S. Office of Technology Assessment (1989, p. 96), "Nearly two thirds of the teleteachers surveyed (64 percent) had not received training prior to teaching over their respective distance learning systems." Many distance education technologies, such as computer-based audiographics systems and videoconferencing, demand strong visuals to support the audio messages. Most classroom educators are not trained or skilled in visualizing content or producing effective visuals.

Many institutions focus large resources on the purchase and implementation of technology systems. Often, if too few funds are earmarked for ongoing orientation and training, faculty will be disgruntled and systems will be underutilized. If distance education is to help improve the quality of education, it will require more educators who use technology well.

Competition for Scarce Dollars. Hardware and transmission costs are dropping, but distance education delivery systems remain capital-intensive. Spending restraints and greater competition for the education dollar will increasingly require joint consortia between higher education and the private sector. While funding for initial purchases is often the easiest, institutions will also face recurring operational, program development, and production costs, as well as capital upgrades. Faculty will be called on to put these new distance education systems into context for administrators and budget officers, as well as demonstrate their continuing educational value and cost-effectiveness.

Keeping Up with Change. Technologies will change, but faculty can begin now to become knowledgeable about distance education research, issues, and successful and unsuccessful applications. By reading, attending conferences, and participating in demonstrations and staff development opportunities delivered via technology, educators can evaluate which distance education systems can meet specific applications.

Participation in Policy-Making. Growing distance education applications and technology alternatives are forcing many states and universities to reexamine policies, rules, and regulations that were written in the context of traditional educational settings. Educators will need to be involved in discussions and policy recommendations regarding distance education course accreditation, teacher certification, public-private partnerships, faculty rewards, and intellectual property concerns, among other issues.

Vendor Relations. Many telecommunications service and equipment vendors are paying increased attention to the education marketplace. Educators should continue to pressure these companies for the services, equipment features, and implementation timelines required to meet specific distance education needs. Finally, educators should demand to put vendor equipment through many hours of use, under actual instructional conditions, before any contracts are awarded.

The Future

Crystal-ball gazing is always risky. But several statements can be made with great certainty: Technology will play a greater role in distance education than ever before; clientele groups will be more diverse in age, culture, skills, expertise, and experience; changes in workplaces and the times will place increasingly greater demands on program personnel to deliver education when and where it's needed (IBM Corporation, 1990).

One corporate plan provides for "distributed" education. Education will take place at individual computer workstations. "Classes" will meet electronically through video or computer conferencing. Electronic mail will be the vehicle for giving and completing assignments. Information will be retrieved online using the computer's power to access remote data bases. According to the plan, "Electronic classmates [will] develop the same shared memories, allegiance, and friendships as students in physical class-rooms" (IBM Corporation, p. iv, 1990).

Will distributed education (Kearsley, 1985) be embraced as the model for distance education of the future? If so, learners will then have the best of distance education worlds: true convenience in terms of time and place, flexibility of self-paced learning, and two-way communication that most learners find essential to the learning process.

Summary and Conclusion

How fast new applications are implemented will depend on many factors, including economic realities. In recent surveys, college officials and law-makers across the country predict that their states' dismal financial con-ditions will overwhelm all of the issues affecting higher education in the near future.

Tight money situations, however, are precisely the driving force behind the efforts of many institutions to find innovative ways to provide equitable education. As Hezel (1992) points out in his nationwide survey, states and institutions are often choosing telecommunications systems to provide answers to this problem.

Today, many universities are evaluating or reevaluating their commit-ment to distance education and the concomitant investment of resources; others are redirecting scarce resources and restructuring themselves around distance education requirements for today and tomorrow. This is not a time to stand still.

References

Brand, S. *The Media Lab: Inventing the Future at MIT.* New York: Viking Penguin, 1987.

Carl, D. R. "Developing Faculty to Use Teleconferencing to Deliver University Credit Courses Over Cable and Satellite." *Canadian Journal of Educational Communication,* 1986, 15 (4), 235–250.

Charles, J. "Adaptations of Distance Education in the 1990s." *ITCA Teleconferencing Yearbook,* 1991, pp. 41–48.

Gehlauf, D. N., Shatz, M. A., and Frye, T. W. "Faculty Perceptions of Interactive Television Instructional Strategies: Implications for Training." *American Journal of Distance Education,* 1991, 5 (3), 20–28.

Hezel, R. T. *Planning for Educational Telecommunications: A State-by-State Analysis, 1992.* Syra-cuse, N.Y.: Hezel Associates, 1992.

Holmberg, B. *Theory and Practice of Distance Education.* New York: Routledge & Kegan Paul, 1989.

IBM Corporation. *A Vision of IBM Human Resource Performance in the Year 2000.* IBM Corporate Education Report. Armonk, N.Y.: IBM, 1990.

Kearsley, G. *Training for Tomorrow.* Reading, Mass.: Addison-Wesley, 1985.

Keegan, D. *The Foundations of Distance Education.* London, England: Croom Helm, 1986.

Monson, M. K. *Bridging the Distance.* Madison: University of Wisconsin-Extension, 1978.

Moore, M. "Toward a Theory of Independent Learning and Teaching." *Journal of Higher Education,* 1973, *44* (12), 661–679.

Smith, P. "Distance Education and Educational Change." In P. Smith and M. Kelly (eds.), *Distance Education and the Mainstream: Convergence in Education.* London, England: Croom Helm, 1987.

Smith, P., and Kelly, M. (eds.). *Distance Education and the Mainstream: Convergence in Education.* London, England: Croom Helm, 1987.

United States Distance Learning Association. "USDLA Holds Congressional Briefing Session: Presents National Policy Recommendations." In *USDLA Annual Report, 1991.* San Ramon, Calif.: Applied Business teleCommunications, 1991.

U.S. Office of Technology Assessment. *Linking for Learning: A New Course for Education.* OTA-SET-430. Washington, D.C.: Government Printing Office, 1989.

Verduin, J. R., Jr., and Clark, T. A. *Distance Education: The Foundations of Effective Practice.* San Francisco: Jossey-Bass, 1991.

Wedemeyer, C. A. *Learning at the Back Door.* Madison: University of Wisconsin Press, 1981.

Zigerell, J. *The Uses of Television in American Higher Education.* New York: Praeger, 1991.

MARCIA A. BAIRD *is director of Instructional Communications Systems (ICS), University of Wisconsin-Extension, Madison. ICS manages audio, audiographic, and videoconferencing distance education delivery systems.*

MAVIS K. MONSON *is associate professor and instructional design manager for ICS.*

Virtual reality is a three-dimensional, participatory, multisensory, computer-based environment that occurs in real time. When applied to instruction, it has the potential to revolutionize teaching and learning processes.

The Emerging Potential of Virtual Reality in Postsecondary Education

James P. Randall

Imagine a laboratory where young medical students practice surgical techniques, making incisions, removing and replacing organs, and experimenting with different decisions, all without the need for a human cadaver.

Picture an architecture student "walking through" a design for a new home with a client, who may not even be present at the same location. From "inside" the home, the architect and client can raise ceilings, move doorways and windows to improve the view, and enlarge, change the configuration of, or even add or delete rooms. The client can check the kitchen design, open cabinet doors to test for obstructions, prepare a dinner to try out the appliance arrangement, and even set the table. All this is done in an electronic simulation.

Think about a biochemistry student "walking around" inside a molecule to better understand its structure and its properties, or an aeronautical engineering student "flying" an experimental plane and experiencing firsthand the effects of making design modifications.

Learning experiences such as these illustrate the promise of virtual reality for higher education. Virtual reality will take students beyond the largely passive environment of the lecture hall and even past the pencil-and-paper simulations of many homework assignments. It will provide hands-on, realistic situations that simulate the real-world environment as closely as possible while minimizing danger to the students and their patients or clients. These experiences will enable students to learn more quickly and thoroughly, while providing insight into the course material that is impossible to obtain in any other way.

The examples cited above are not mere speculations. They are illus-

New Directions for Teaching and Learning, no. 51, Fall 1992 © Jossey-Bass Publishers

trations of experiments already in progress at prestigious universities such as Stanford, Northwestern, and the Universities of Washington and North Carolina at Chapel Hill. Although few students are able to experience virtual reality today, the technology will become more available as the decade progresses. Still, virtual reality is not likely to have any significant impact on college teaching until early in the twenty-first century.

What Is Virtual Reality?

Virtual reality (VR), also called *artificial reality* or *cyberspace,* is an emerging technology with important implications not only for the practice of teaching and learning but for their conceptualization as well. Employing three-dimensional computer graphics, high resolution display technology, and multisensory, interactive interface devices, VR immerses the user in a simulated world that closely reflects how humans naturally operate in the real world.

VR is participatory. When experiencing a virtual environment, the user feels as if he or she is actually there. A virtual environment can be real or imaginary, abstract or concrete. VR has the potential to provide learning experiences that are hands-on, group or individualized, that simulate reality and occur in real time. Bricken (1991, p. 178) suggests that "within the limits of system functionality, we can create anything imaginable and then become part of it." This is full conceptual and perceptual participation in a potential learning environment.

VR is multisensory. Computer-generated images displayed on tiny, eye-covering, head-mounted screens result in the perception of three-dimensional imagery. Data glove technology allows the individual to "feel" virtual objects. Force feedback mechanisms provide an added element of realism to tactile interaction. A full body suit allows the wearer to interact kinesthetically within a virtual environment.

VR occurs in real time. Interaction in a virtual environment, as a reflection of physical reality, happens in much the same way as interaction in real-world time and space, except that the experience is computer generated.

Virtual Reality Technology

Technological requirements for achieving virtual environments include three-dimensional computer graphics in a graphical user interface, multisensory interactive interface devices, high-resolution displays, and high-level computing power in workstation environments. Most existing VR systems require the power of a supercomputer, although advances in computer technology may eventually permit VR systems to be operated by desktop or even portable computers (Puttre, 1991).

Human interface with the computer is achieved through a network of sensors attached to the operator. The DataGlove developed by VPL Research is made of lycra material and is fitted with multiple sensors that monitor finger and hand movements. When connected to a computer through fiber-optic cables, data imputed by the sensors in the glove enable the computer to generate an on-screen image that precisely follows the operator's hand movements. The glove also provides tactile feedback to the operator through the use of miniature force feedback mechanisms in its fingertips.

VPL Research's DataSuit is a full-body garment that is worn by the user, enabling full-body interaction with the virtual environment. Head-mounted displays provide high-resolution, stereoscopic display screens for each eye, thus providing the visual illusion of multidimensionality of the visual field. Stereo audio is also delivered to the headset, which enhances the realism of the VR experience.

As might be expected, cost is presently a prohibitive factor in the development and adoption of VR technology. Given the requirements for computing power and the level of sophistication of peripheral equipment, workstations presently range from $25,000 to $250,000 at the low end, and between $750,000 and $1 million for each high-end system.

Current Research and Development in Virtual Reality

In addition to the experimental work described above, current application areas for VR systems include entertainment, distance communication, telepresence, visualization and simulation, and training (Grimes, 1991). Building on the enormous popularity of video games, VR technology has the potential for transforming the nature of entertainment (Bylinsky, 1991). Virtual Worlds Entertainment's "Battletech Multi-Player Virtual World Simulator" is an entertainment application in which each player navigates a BattleMech, a thirty-foot-tall human-shaped fighting tank, over one hundred miles of computer-generated terrain. The cockpits in which the players sit contain over one hundred input-output devices, including primary and secondary screen displays, foot pedals, joysticks, throttles, light emitting diode (LED) displays and switches.

A multi-unit entertainment system was recently installed in Chicago, in which teams test their tactical skills and strategies by engaging in battles over alien terrain. Other entertainment applications include Fake Space Labs' "Be Here Now," a series of virtual explorations; Naimark & Company's "EAT— A Virtual Dining Environment" and "VBK—A Moviemap of Karlsruhe," which address dining and travel, respectively; and Mr. Film's "Performance Cartoons," including Silver Surfer and Silver Suzy surfing experiences.

Nonentertainment systems, however, are more illustrative of the potential of VR for higher education. For example, distance communication and telepresence applications include Vivid Effects's "Mandala Teleconferencing

System," which allows people in different cities to be seen and have their live images projected into a mutual real-time, virtual world, where they can interactively control aspects of their virtual experience together.

SimGraphics's "AAAP Assembly Modeler" is a visualization application permitting users to manipulate graphically rendered objects as they would maneuver real parts during actual use in manufacturing and maintenance. In a similar manner, Boeing's "VSX" system allows aircraft designers to visualize and evaluate design performance in terms of an aircraft's operability, maintainability, and manufacturability.

Among simulation and training applications, the Naval Postgraduate School has developed "NPSNET," a real-time, three-dimensional system simulating vehicle movement over the ground or in the air. Displays show roads, buildings, soil types, and elevations. The system is also capable of incorporating environmental effects such as fog or smog, vehicles, houses, trees, signs, and animals. The viewer then selects a vehicle and drives it through this virtual environment.

Other simulation and training applications include Silicon Graphics's "Plasm: Above the Drome," an exploration environment in which the viewer can pursue exploring, athletic styling, systematic treasure hunting, and game creating and playing. Researchers at the University of North Carolina at Chapel Hill have developed "Radiation Therapy," which allows the user to target radiation beams and position them to pass through tumors, while avoiding as much healthy tissue as possible.

In addition to the organizations identified above, research-and-development pioneers include Artificial Reality's Myron Krueger, who established much of the groundwork for VR systems in *Artificial Reality* (Krueger, 1983); VPL Research's Jaron Lanier, who originated the term *virtual reality;* University of North Carolina at Chapel Hill's Frederick Brooks; and departments at NASA's Ames Research Center and the Human Interface Technology Laboratory at the University of Washington.

The literature on VR is primarily found in engineering and applied science data bases, with journals such as *IEEE Computer Graphics and Applications, Computer Graphics, Compressed Air,* and *New Science and Mechanical Engineering* among those reporting applications of this emerging technology. The journal *Virtual Reality Report and Multimedia Review* debuted in 1990, and conferences on VR have been sponsored by the Association for Computer Machinery's Special Interest Group-Graphics (ACM SIGGRAPH) and Mechler in the past three years. Recent research and development reports are also found on Bitnet and Internet, with electronic mail postings to VR message interest groups and "lists" serving as the primary information dissemination media.

Conclusion

As noted earlier, VR is an emerging technology with potentially revolutionary possibilities for teaching and learning. The literature certainly indicates that the technology has great potential in training, simulation, and the creation of full learning environments (Fritz, 1991; Bricken, 1991; Randall, 1992). However, at present it is a prototypical technology with only a limited but expanding group of developers working in the field of education.

Dialogue needs to be initiated to formulate a national agenda for implementation and impact of VR on higher education. Questions must be formulated relative to curriculum, learning environment design, implementation and evaluation, as well as teaching roles, ethics, social responsibility, and cost in using this technology in colleges and universities. Leadership at the postsecondary level needs to capture the vision of the potential of this extraordinary new technology.

References

Bricken, M. "Virtual Reality Learning Environments: Potentials and Challenges." *Computer Graphics,* 1991, *25* (3), 178–184.

Bylinsky, G. "The Marvels of 'Virtual Reality.'" *Fortune,* June 3, 1991, pp. 138–150.

Fritz, M. "The World of Virtual Reality." *Training,* 1991, *28* (2), 45–50.

Grimes, J. "Virtual Reality '91 Anticipates Future Reality." *IEEE Computer Graphics and Applications,* 1991, *11*, 81–83.

Krueger, M. W. *Artificial Reality.* Reading, Mass.: Addison-Wesley, 1983.

Puttre, M. "Virtual Reality Comes into Focus." *Mechanical Engineering,* 1991, *113* (4), 56–59.

Randall, J. P. "Virtual Reality: Capture the Vision." Paper presented at the annual conference of the Association for Educational Communications and Technology, Washington, D.C., February 1992.

JAMES P. RANDALL is assistant professor of instructional technology at the Center for Education, Widener University, Chester, Pennsylvania, and president and chief executive officer of the RANTECH Group, Lansdowne, Pennsylvania.

How will the research library be transformed by the Information Age? What place will the research library have in the university of the twenty-first century? Will we even need a library in twenty-five years?

The Research Library and Emerging Information Technology

Lucy Siefert Wegner

For many in academia, the word *library* evokes visions of quiet, book-lined rooms, whispering librarians, and long hours of toil through dusty tomes. Libraries are cathedrals of knowledge, housing humankind's accumulated knowledge for the use of reverent readers. Collections are treasures to be guarded, with librarians the guardians.

One result of this view is that many university faculty rarely use the library at their institution. To find information, they consult with colleagues or use bibliographies and footnotes. When in great need, they send assistants to the library in their stead. As a result, there is a widespread unawareness of the services that the library offers, and little appreciation of what the library is becoming in the electronic age (Dougherty, 1992).

What Is Happening to the Tried and True?

Scholars and teachers in today's highly automated and pressured society need convenient access (read, "in my office"), at convenient times (late night and weekends), and in convenient form, whether audio, video, or computer data base. These needs will only increase in the next decade as more advanced information tools become available.

Electronic technology has changed the way that we live our lives, the way that classes are taught, and the way that students study and learn. The Information Age brought with it an information explosion, and all scholarship has felt its effects. It is increasingly difficult to keep abreast of developments in one's area of expertise, much less in a broad field of knowledge. In addition to familiar books and journals, information is now clothed in new forms: data bases, multimedia packages, online bulletin boards, "list-servs," and remote resources available on computer networks.

Libraries are torn between the old and the new, without the means to do justice to both. The cost of maintaining traditional print collections and resources is becoming prohibitive. In the ten years between 1979 and 1989, prices for books and journals rose 216 percent (measured in 1979 dollars). Prices for library materials are rising faster than the consumer price index. In 1990, the consumer price index was 6.1 percent, but prices for periodicals (journals and magazines) rose 9.5 percent and prices for academic books rose 7.2 percent (Halstead, 1991).

Even if it were possible to maintain collections as in the past, new technologies and resources have arisen that did not even exist five years ago. Room must be made for huge online data bases, multimedia products, and user-centered access systems. The cost of adding these new technologies and services cannot be estimated, but it is certain to be breathtaking.

This much is certain: Libraries cannot continue to be structured and operated as they have been in the past. In order to remain vital centers of learning and study for universities, research libraries must redefine and reinvent themselves. Otherwise, they may be relegated to service as book museums or archives. As Lyman (1991, p. 41) writes, "Either we must be willing to pay a great deal more to preserve traditional scholarly habits, such as browsing in stacks, or the scholarly community must adopt radically new modes of storing and accessing information."

Alternatives to Print

Libraries have responded to the opportunities of the Information Age, and they are now one of the two places in modern life where we will almost certainly use a computer, the other being the bank. Online finding tools enable the library user to compile a list of desired material and then determine where the material is located. These computerized indexes and catalogs offer many advantages: combination of terms, access to any word in the record, and speed.

Computer-Based Online Public Access Catalogs (OPACs). OPACs have eliminated the overhead of filing innumerable cards in catalog drawers and also have made possible far more precise retrieval. For example, suppose I wish to find books that deal with crime prevention in public housing. With a card catalog, it would be difficult or impossible to ferret out items that deal with both topics. First, I must look up one subject, then the other, and try to scan the entries. When I look at the online catalog here at my university, there are 247 items with the subject heading Public Housing, and 339 with the subject heading Crime Prevention. On the computer, I can easily look for items that have both of these subject headings and find the four that match.

Periodical Indexes in Digital Form. In the last ten years, periodical indexes, long a staple of research in their print form, have been converted to digital form and made available in libraries through dialing to a vendor service (such as Dialog or Bibliographic Retrieval Services [BRS]), installation of compact disk-read only memory (CD-ROM) systems, and local mounting of data base tapes on a mainframe computer.

In ten years, the periodical index system will be a pedagogical tool to guide and train the user. The student will type (or speak, as these systems may very well understand spoken commands) the words, "I need information on outer space." The system will respond, "Is there some aspect of outer space that particularly interests you?" (*not* "Outer space—set too large, try again. OK"). This scenario is reminiscent of the fake psychologist computer programs that are so amusing ("What don't you like about your mother?"), but even this kind of prompting can help new users focus their search strategies. The system could be even more directive and query the user, "Are you more interested in physiological or psychological effects of weightlessness?" Based on the user's response, the system would suggest or even choose appropriate resources.

Additionally, item records will be enriched. When cards had to be typed and filed, there was a premium on brevity, and restrictions on how many subjects to assign to an item. Similarly, indexes to periodical literature used broad topics for an article to make it easy to find in a print volume.

With a computer-based catalog, these restrictions no longer apply. Now the table of contents, chapter headings, titles and authors of individual chapters, abstracts, and as many subject headings as are needed to describe the content of the item in detail can be added.

The item record will be just the beginning. From there, the seeker will be able to move to an abstract, read the full text of the article or book, and view illustrations, graphs, and charts. Articles may have audio or moving pictures connected to them. The user could ask for an article or part of a book to be printed on demand, fully formatted, with layout and illustrations as in the printed version.

Microforms. Microform technology has been a boon for libraries with little space to spare. Whether microfilm reels, fiche, or cards, this technology has become the preferred method to preserve back issues of journals, out-of-print books, and historical collections. Microformats are not popular with library users, however. Complaints range from "impossible to read" to "hard to print." At this time, there is no more efficient, economical, or longer-lasting format.

CD-ROM. Some hail the advent of CD-ROM or laser disks as a replacement for microformats, but it is not yet known for how long the disks remain stable and readable. The problem is not only physical degradation (the silver coating can peel away from the plastic backing), but also changes in access technology. Almost every library has an example of materials that are unreadable ten years later because of advances in technology.

Media Centers. Libraries have long collected audiovisual materials and made them available in media centers. Until now, these have been discrete items, with little or no integration as coherent teaching tools. There may be film of the rituals of a tribal group, recordings of their music, and the field notes of an anthropologist, but no way to tie them all together.

The next ten years will see development of computer software packages that combine sound and pictures (from a CD-ROM), study material, and evaluation modules. These programs will reinforce material covered in class lectures and provide detailed reviews. Students will study at their own pace on their own time, going over the material as many times as needed.

Net Result in Today's Library. At today's university, a student researching a paper may consult one computer system to ascertain what the library owns on a subject, consult a CD-ROM index to find journal articles, look up the articles on microfilm, and perhaps view a videotape on the research topic. These tasks could very well take the student all over the building, if not all over campus. In the future library, it may be possible to do all this at one workstation, with all of the resources at the student's fingertips.

The Configuration of Tomorrow's Library

In tomorrow's library, students and researchers will be able to find and retrieve a variety of materials without leaving their desks. In addition to shelves of materials and study areas, computer workstations will be integral parts of the library's infrastructure, as common as desk chairs.

The Virtual Library. In ten years, the library that we know today will be augmented by virtual libraries, which "are collections of materials about which a user can learn through systems developed by the library, and which the library can then obtain for the user" (Lynch, 1991, p. 77). Resources that seem to be locally available will actually be held at remote locations. Lynch adds that "access to the library's holdings will be primarily electronic" (p. 78).

A library's holdings will be defined by access, not by possession. Much of the library's material will be delivered in electronic form, or printed on demand. There will be "some inherently electronic objects that cannot be examined except through computers and networks," and when the library user accesses these electronic resources, the system will "enforce intellectual property rights and, if appropriate, collect royalties" (Lynch, 1991, p. 78).

Faculty and students will no longer be tied to the resources that the library owns in physical form. Granted, scholars now can request items through interlibrary loan services, if they have the time and foresight to do so. But faculty members cannot easily require students to read something that the library does not own. With the virtual library, faculty and students will be free to use any resource to which the library has *access*.

How will these services sit with library users? "There are many problems with this scenario, not least that library patrons like browsing in the physical stacks, and that collection size is a primary measure of status in the competition between institutions" (Lyman, 1991, p. 40). The criteria for excellence will need to change, as well as users' expectations.

National and International Computer Networks. Virtual libraries, and users in their own homes, will access resources through expanded high-speed electronic networks. Vast amounts of data will move quickly across the network, including pictures and graphics.

As illustrative indications of the importance and complexity of the networks now being developed, two projects warrant mention. The National Research and Education Network (NREN) was created by the federal High-Performance Computing Act of 1991. It will be "a framework for coordinating and leveraging the networking programs of agencies of the Federal Government, a program for engineering and deploying billion-bit-per-second and higher performance networks, and a process for formulating and evaluating public policy" (Peters, 1992). The Coalition for Networked Information (CNI), a joint project of the Association of Research Libraries, CAUSE (formerly, College and University Systems Exchange), and EDUCOM (Interuniversity Communications Council), has fifty-four member institutions and organizations. CNI seeks to facilitate progress toward the development of advanced networks to support new modes of scholarly activity. It is also strongly committed to the development of global access to resources in order to avoid creation of an information elite in developed nations.

Resources of the Virtual Library. The new networks will carry familiar forms of data and also new forms of information:

Electronic Journals. There has been tremendous growth recently in the number of journals that are available only in electronic form. Some of these are peer reviewed, such as *Psycoloquy* and *Current Clinical Trials*, which are a joint project of the American Association for the Advancement of Science and the Online Computer Library Center (OCLC).

Huge Data Bases. We are now seeing the collection of masses of information that can only be conceived and accessed by electronic means. An example is the Human Genome Project (Courteau, 1991). This group of data bases will eventually list the location of every one of the genome's over one-hundred thousand genes. Over eight hundred megabytes (approximately two hundred and fifty thousand to three hundred thousand pages) of data have already been collected, and the project is less than one-third complete.

Full Text. In addition to journals on the network, other types of texts will also be available. For example, Project Gutenberg has the goal of encouraging "the creation and distribution of electronic text" (Hart, 1992). The project hopes to have ten thousand "etexts" (texts in electronic form) in distribution by the end of the year 2001. A small sampling of the texts that are now available includes *Alice in Wonderland, Declaration of Independence, CIA World Factbook, Book of Mormon,* and *Moby Dick.*

Net Result in the Virtual Library. In the new scenario, the professor preparing a lecture will access materials from the library, including sound, images, and simulations. He or she selects background material to recommend to the students for study or drill. All of these items are then sent to the professor's desk for review.

In turn, a student goes to the library to review the material selected by the professor and also to study with a group of other students. The student begins research for a term paper by performing an online search of the library's catalog, periodical indexes, other libraries' catalogs, and full-text data bases. The finished paper will include some film clips pulled from the library's video archive. This term paper and other assignments will be sent to the professor electronically.

Concluding Questions

Movement from the current state of libraries to the grand future will be an enormous task. It will not happen easily or without careful thought. There are no "right" answers to these questions, but they must be addressed.

Will the Library Disappear? Will it be a location, or a virtual reality? A repository or a resource? What will be left for the library to house? What will be its function? "The day may come when libraries as we know them become museums of materials that predate this truly electronic age, and serve as repositories of books for recreational reading" (Ra, 1991, p. 25).

The library will continue, but it will be transformed. It will be home to resources that are too new, expensive, complex, or arcane to be used outside its walls. It will house the access technology and the staff to run it. It will be a center of cooperative learning, with group work areas, auditoriums, and demonstration areas.

It will house the books.

Will the Book Disappear? If the book is viewed as a technology and not as a particular physical form, it is clear that the book, or something like it, will always be used. The guiding principle is to use the appropriate technology for a particular purpose.

Print materials have many qualities that recommend them. They are completely portable and need no outside power source. They offer truly random access to their contents and require no special training or knowledge to use. They combine text and visual material in a seamless whole. They are inexpensive to produce and durable. The format has been refined through the centuries and has stood the test of centuries of use.

What Will Be the Role of Librarians? Librarians are resource and access specialists. The librarian will be a teacher and guide to the expanding universe of information, showing the order in the chaos.

Fulfillment of this role will require the development of new methods of assisting library users. "The librarian may also serve as a bridge between the traditional and the new, serving the needs of the less educated by mediating, teaching, and bringing them up to a level where they can become part of the electronic age" (Ra, 1991, p. 26). But, how will the librarian find, reach, educate, and support users who are not even in the building? Will some users get lost in a seemingly endless maze of data bases?

What Will Be the Role of Library Users? Five years ago, librarians would perform online searches for patrons. With the proliferation of resources and the ability of users to access resources from their own offices (remotely), the trend is for users to perform their own searches. However, a beginning information seeker has difficulty in four areas of information retrieval:

Articulating a Request. It is a truism in library circles that users never ask for what they really want. For example, an information seeker may ask for books on outer space. It may take skill and time from the librarian to find that what the user really wants are articles on the physiological effects of extended periods of weightlessness.

Choosing the Appropriate Data Base. Pick a topic and a multitude of online resources are available: catalogs, bibliographic indexes, research data, guides, and full-text files. The inexperienced user, or even one who is experienced but in an unfamiliar subject area, may find choosing the correct resource a daunting task.

Vocabulary and Format. Presently, the searcher must learn each particular data base and system, with all of their idiosyncrasies. A particular data base may feature classification codes, or an elaborate hierarchy of search terms to make retrieval easier, but all of these features must be learned in order to perform a precise, efficient search. The interface to the data base (what the user sees on the screen) may have its own protocols and methods. If a library has several of these resources, the hapless user must try to learn several ways to access the data.

Interpretation of Results. The retrieved list may be two or two thousand items in length. The user must analyze the results and decide the next step. Should the search be broader or narrower? Should the user browse this list and pick relevant material? And what does the record mean? Where can the user find the material now that he or she knows it exists?

Information Literacy. In addition to all of the materials that we now teach, tomorrow's students will also need to be taught to be information literate. They will need data base navigation skills that were once the exclusive province of librarians and other information experts. This student need means that faculty must be information literate as well.

The American Library Association (1989, p. 1) defines information literacy as being "able to recognize when information is needed and have the ability to locate, evaluate, and use effectively the needed information. . . . Ultimately, information literate people are those who have learned how to learn."

Who among us can count themselves truly information literate? In order to function effectively in the intellectual climate of the future, all segments of the academic community will have to rely on each other for training, assistance, and encouragement in the task of lifelong learning.

And so, the old vision of the library must be replaced. The new vision involves students, faculty, researchers, and librarians, all working toward the creation of an information literate society that recognizes the library, in whatever physical or virtual form, as a resource for information, old or new. Libraries must change, but so too must the academic community. Together, they can take the university into the next century.

References

American Library Association Presidential Committee on Information Literacy. *Final Report.* Chicago: American Library Association, 1989.

Courteau, J. "Genome Databases." *Science,* 1991, *254*, 201–207.

Dougherty, R. M. "Needed: User-Responsive Research Libraries." *Library Journal,* 1992, *116* (19), 59–62.

Halstead, K. "Library Price Indexes for Colleges and Schools." In F. Simora (ed.), *Bowker Annual Library and Book Trade Almanac.* New York: Bowker, 1991.

Hart, M. S. "Blurb." Message posted on the Project Gutenberg E-Mail List (GUTNBERG@UI-UCVMD), Feb. 8, 1992.

Lyman, P. "The Library of the (Not-So-Distant) Future." *Change,* 1991, *23* (1), 34–41.

Lynch, C. A. "Visions of Electronic Libraries." In F. Simora (ed.), *Bowker Annual Library and Book Trade Almanac.* New York: Bowker, 1991.

Peters, P. E. "CNI Newsletter-Part 1." Message posted on the Public Access Computer Systems Forum (PACS-L@UHUPVM1), Jan. 8, 1992.

Ra, M. "The Future of Resource Sharing: Is There Any?" *Computers in Libraries,* 1991, *11* (2), 25–26.

LUCY SIEFERT WEGNER is head of library automation development at the Center for Scholarly Technology, University of Southern California, Los Angeles.

Although campuswide media centers provide essential services to faculty and students, frequently they are not given the opportunity to operate effectively.

The Future of Campus Media Centers

Michael J. Albright

As recently as the 1960s, when many of our senior faculty members and administrators were beginning their academic careers, large, centralized media centers held a virtual monopoly on technology-based instructional support services. They circulated and repaired media equipment, produced films and handmade graphics, managed film collections, and maintained closed-circuit television systems (CCTV). Instructional applications of computing were still in the experimental stage. Most libraries were interested only in nonprint collections. Distance education consisted mainly of correspondence courses and a few live classes presented on broadcast television. Instructional and faculty development centers did not appear until the end of the decade. Telephone services were the province of the local phone company.

The evolution of instructional and information technology has brought major changes to college teaching and its related support structure. Computers have emerged as the dominant instructional technology format of the 1990s, with academic computing centers the locus of most computer-related services. The greatest expertise in another important new format, optical disk technology, is likely to be found in the library, not the media center. Personal computers, "prosumer" video equipment, and authoring software have become so common and easy to use that many graphics and video production projects are done "in house" by academic units and individual faculty members. Indeed, academic units sometimes have more highly skilled personnel and better equipment than are available at the media center. CCTV systems are being replaced by fiber-optic video and data networks, managed by computing centers or offices of information technology.

NEW DIRECTIONS FOR TEACHING AND LEARNING, no. 51, Fall 1992 © Jossey-Bass Publishers

Many centers providing campuswide media services have adjusted well to this unprecedented period of change. They have embraced new technologies and services and are supporting and collaborating with faculty, academic departments, and other campuswide service agencies to integrate these new learning systems into the curricula. Some media centers, however, cling to their audiovisual orientation and regard other instructional support offices as competitors instead of collaborators. On still other campuses, instructional technology has been given little opportunity to have an impact; media support services, if they exist at all, are placed subordinate to administrators with no accountability for effective teaching, given minimal budgets, and managed by paraprofessionals.

Scope of Instructional Technology

To understand the roles that a campus media center might and should play, it is helpful to place these services within the context of a college or university's broader instructional technology support program. The term *instructional technology* is much misunderstood. It is not the current jargon for films and projectors, nor is it a convenient synonym for academic computing. Instructional technology is a much broader concept that includes virtually every aspect of the teaching and learning process. The Association for Educational Communications and Technology (1977) identified the basic concerns of instructional technology as the messages, people, materials, devices, techniques, and settings that are utilized to bring about learning. Thus, the domain of instructional technology includes not only media and computer equipment services but also materials development, including computer and multimedia software, campuswide distribution systems, curriculum development and instructional problem solving, enhancement of teaching skills among faculty members, and even oversight responsibilities for the classroom environment.

My Integrated Instructional Technology Services model (Albright, 1989) reflects this broad mission of instructional technology in a higher education setting. The model identifies seven basic functional areas, most of which exist in one form or another on virtually every college and university campus: (1) *Learning Resources*, the collections of learning materials, both print and nonprint, for faculty and student use; (2) *Classroom Technologies*, involving media equipment-related services, campuswide distribution systems, and environmental scanning of classrooms; (3) *Media Development*, the systematic design and production of instructional materials and related systems; (4) *Instructional and Faculty Development*, the consulting services that help faculty members solve specific instructional problems and improve general teaching skills; (5) *Academic Computing*, the services supporting the instructional use of computers; (6) *Instructional Telecommunications*, the management of or liaison with systems used to deliver educational programs to off-campus students; and (7) *Research and Evaluation,* services such as course and instructor evaluation, test scoring, and consultation on classroom research.

Responsibility for the many services falling into these categories has become quite fragmented on most college and university campuses. In addition to the centralized media center, players may include the academic library, computing center, office of information technology, faculty development center, office of continuing education, campus television center, and specialized media centers operated by academic departments and colleges. Rarely will a single campus agency have primary responsibility for more than four or five functional areas, and most will provide just one or two.

Media centers typically offer Classroom Technologies services at a minimum. Most provide Media Development and Learning Resources services, some offer Instructional (but rarely Faculty) Development assistance, and a few on campuses with active distance education programs provide Instructional Telecommunications support. Only in isolated cases are these units active in the Academic Computing and the Research and Evaluation functional areas. Most of those centers that provide Instructional and Faculty Development, Academic Computing, and/or Research and Evaluation services have titles reflecting this broader mission, such as Center for Instructional Support or Office of Academic Services.

Emerging Roles of the Campus Media Center

The following are descriptions of some of the more important roles that centralized media centers can be expected to play in the 1990s.

Consultation Services. Perhaps the single most important service is consultation with faculty members regarding the effective integration of technology into their courses. Media center personnel who have an in-depth understanding of college teaching processes and stay abreast of new developments in their field are in an excellent position to help faculty bring innovative and highly effective refinements to their teaching.

Equipment-Related Services. On some campuses, media equipment is regarded as frills or toys for the faculty. A more accurate analogy is that media represents the tools of the trade for the teaching profession, as vital to faculty members as are computers to travel agents and scientific calculators to engineers. Professors *can* teach without media equipment, and many do, but few will be teaching without some form of technology in the twenty-first century. Although the technologies will change, the function of acquiring, distributing, and maintaining them will remain an important instructional technology service area.

Some media centers have placed high-demand items, such as video playback units, video-data projection systems, and overhead and slide projectors, in satellite equipment pools located in classroom buildings in order to make them more easily accessible to the faculty. A related trend is toward establishment of multimedia-equipped classrooms, selected according to size and campus location and scheduled on a semester basis by those classes with greatest need for the technologies. Multimedia classrooms are discussed in greater detail by Lamb (this volume).

Concern for Classroom Environment. On many campuses, no single office has taken responsibility for monitoring and improving the environment for teaching and learning in classrooms. This is a basic instructional technology function that is now routinely assigned to media centers. This mission includes periodic inspection of classroom facilities, including chalkboards, seating, lighting, window darkening devices, projection screens, and overall cleanliness, and work with physical plant personnel to resolve deficiencies. Some centers have now established campus hot lines to field and resolve complaints from faculty members and students regarding classroom facilities.

Concern for Classroom Design. Poorly designed classrooms are an unfortunate fact of life at many colleges and universities. Instructional technology personnel should be present during the initial planning stages of all new construction and building renovation projects to serve as advocates for effective classroom design. Typical areas of concern include orientation of classrooms so that doors are in the rear, student view angles, acoustical treatment, lighting controls, AC power demands and placement of outlets, external noise control, size and placement of chalkboards, and provisions for the installation of equipment such as a video-data projector, screen, sound system, and remote controls.

Video and Multimedia Production and Consultation Services. Videotape remains an extremely popular format for instructional support materials. The emergence of high-quality, relatively low-cost portable video recording equipment and computer-based editing systems has made sophisticated video production capabilities quite affordable for most college campuses. The development of custom-made videotapes meeting specific instructional needs will be an important media center service area for many years to come.

With the proliferation of consumer-level electronic equipment and simplification of authoring systems, many faculty members are now engaged in the development of their own multimedia materials. Media center personnel should be available to provide consultation support, as well as to produce video segments that the faculty clients are unable to create for themselves. Moreover, these personnel are likely to serve as the primary developers in many multimedia development projects with faculty members.

Computer Graphics Services. Personal computers and sophisticated graphics software packages have made the production of high-quality slides, overhead transparencies, and hard copies an easily achievable media center service. While many professors are fully capable of creating their own graphics files, many others are not and must rely on a centralized production service. It also makes sense for expensive output devices such as a film recorder (for slides) and color thermal printer (for transparencies and hard copies) to be located in a centralized location, such as the media center. At some institutions, faculty members are able to transfer files through the campus data communications network to the center for printing. These services are described at some length by Head (this volume).

Distance Education Support. On many campuses that provide distance education programs, media centers manage and operate the telecommunications delivery systems, serve as liaison with external agencies, and produce courseware. Distance education support services are discussed in detail by Baird and Monson (this volume).

Instructional Development Services. Offices providing faculty development services often focus on improvement of the general teaching skills of faculty members but are unable to provide expert assistance to professors in solving specific instructional problems. Instructional development services, ranging from curriculum development projects to creation or improvement of single-course assignments, are another basic instructional technology function. These services have significant potential for making college teaching more effective. Yet, ironically, they are offered on only a few campuses, and rarely by individuals with formal training in instructional development methodology.

Other Service Areas. Other important service areas for media centers include consultative assistance to faculty members who are developing proposals for instructional improvement projects, maintenance of videotapes and other learning resources for faculty and student use, satellite reception and off-air recording services, operation of a media equipment pool dedicated to students, audio- and videotape recording and duplicating, equipment repair services, and operation of a self-service materials production center.

Barriers to the Success of Media Centers

At present, instructional technology has never had greater potential for supporting and improving undergraduate education. Yet, it is a fair assessment that this potential is far from being realized. The economic conditions of the early 1990s have limited the ability of colleges and universities to invest in instructional technology and its related support services. However, other factors seem to have played equally important roles in the underutilization of media and other forms of instructional technology on college campuses.

Lack of Recognition. Much national attention has been focused on improvement of undergraduate education and the transformation of college teaching. However, relatively little discussion time has been given to the role of instructional technology in this process. The director of EDUCOM's Educational Uses of Information Technology (EUIT) Project recently complained, in an open letter to leaders of the American Association for Higher Education (AAHE), that computers and other instructional technologies have "disappeared from the horizon" in AAHE conference sessions addressing the future of postsecondary education; he did not feel that technology was being rejected, just never considered (Gilbert, 1990). Even at the campus level, as Konomos (1991) found, directors of media centers perceive that their single most important responsibility is to explain their roles to administrators.

Inappropriate Reporting Structures. Campus media centers have a more widespread and direct effect on faculty success in the classroom than is achieved by any other support service unit. Yet, higher education appears to be in a constant struggle to find the proper administrative location for them. For example, the 1991 annual member survey conducted by the Consortium of College and University Media Centers (1992) found that 53 percent of the responding centers either had been part of administrative reorganizations in the previous five years or expected to be included in campus restructuring in the near future. An analysis of the reassignments suggested that most were for administrative convenience rather than carefully considered efforts to improve services to faculty. No trends were evident.

The primary (and on most campuses exclusive) mission of the media center is to support and enhance the quality of teaching and learning. The center director should therefore report to that individual *who has the greatest amount of accountability for the overall excellence of the institution's instructional program.* That person is the chief academic officer. Only the chief academic officer has a strong *vested interest* in the success of instructional technology support services on a campuswide basis.

A recent survey found that just 34 percent of college and university media center directors nationwide reported to the chief academic officer or an immediate subordinate in that office (Albright, 1991). This percentage was relatively consistent across Carnegie Foundation classifications and private and public institutions. The largest group, 39 percent, reported to the library director or subordinate in the library. The remaining 27 percent reported to a mix of administrators, ranging from academic unit deans to the directors of public relations, business services, student unions, and facilities management.

The high percentage of directors reporting to librarians illustrates administrative misunderstanding of the mission and functions of media centers. The Learning Resources functional area, including nonprint media collections and learning laboratories in which to use them, has long been a legitimate academic library activity. However, other instructional technology services, such as classroom media equipment support, instructional development, and the management of off-campus telecommunications systems, are not normal library functions. (After all, libraries do not write and publish books; why should they be asked to produce videotapes?) This reporting structure has worked effectively only on those campuses where the library director has a vision of instructional technology and the library has partner services dedicated to supporting the educational enterprise of the institution.

In the face of budgetary stress, it is a predictable response for a library director to cut classroom equipment and media production allocations in an attempt to preserve the acquisitions budget and reference services. The impact of this funding loyalty and the generally smaller pool of available resources was evident in the results of my national survey (Albright, 1991) of 189 centers identified as the primary media service providers on their respective campuses. At public, doctorate-granting universities, centers reporting to chief academic officers received a median budget of $1.1 million, while the median budget for centers subordinate to library directors was just $400,000. The study found that chief academic officers provided significantly more funding support at each Carnegie classification level.

A similar funding concern is raised by the current trend toward grouping media services with information technology organizations. Information technology is a blanket term for technologies used to support the processing, storage, retrieval, transfer, and communication of information (D. Lassner, personal communication, August 4, 1991). Instructional technology product-oriented services certainly fall into that category. However, the scope of information technology extends well beyond instructional support and includes research support, administrative computing, data network services, and voice (telephone) communications. Chief information officers can be expected to support academic computing and some distance education functions of instructional technology, but, as with library directors, their commitment to funding and to serving as advocate for classroom equipment services, media production, instructional development, and other services oriented toward instructional improvement is open to question. Of the eight media centers subordinate to information technology organizations in my study (Albright, 1991), four appeared to be seriously underfunded.

Absence of Strong, Effective Leadership. At any institution, but particularly at large universities, the director of the campus media center should spend a substantial amount of his or her time operating at the strategic level. Primary tasks should include helping academic units integrate instructional technology into the curriculum, strategic planning, program development, grant writing and other forms of fund-raising, and promotion and public relations. The director should interact on a daily basis with vice presidents, deans, department chairs, senior professors, university committees and task forces, and other directors of campus units.

Search committees generally do not look for directors who can function effectively at the strategic level. Job descriptions are typically written to emphasize technical knowledge and minimal educational requirements. For example, in 1989–1990, twenty-five advertisements for directors of campuswide media services appeared in the *Chronicle of Higher Education*. Only nine of these positions required graduate degrees in instructional technology, and only one of these specifically required a Ph.D. Just two advertisements identified strategic skills, one of which had only a vague reference. Minimal experience levels were sought. Fifteen of the advertisements required a master's degree in library science and listed librarian skills prominently among the qualifications. Only one advertisement required a record of scholarship.

These low expectations are reflected in the professional credentials and activities of persons who currently direct campuswide media service agencies. In my survey (Albright, 1991), just 21 percent of the responding directors held doctorates, and only 7 percent held Ph.D.s specifically in instructional technology or a closely related field. On the other hand, 6 percent had no college degree at all, and 19 percent held only bachelor's degrees. An additional 23 percent held only master's degrees in library science or nonrelated disciplines. Since the basic degree in instructional technology is a master's degree, it appears that nearly *half* of the college and university media center directors in this country have never completed the minimum educational requirements to *enter the profession,* let alone establish credibility with deans and department chairs. The survey also found that almost 27 percent of the responding directors held no memberships in professional associations, and that for nearly 20 percent the directorship was a part-time position. Less than 35 percent reported holding faculty rank, nearly half of these by virtue of their positions as library staff members.

Deans, department chairs, and senior faculty rarely regard as peers and collaborators those media directors with bachelor's and even master's degrees, who do not hold faculty rank, and who do not teach, conduct research, publish, secure grants, or actively participate in university governance. The director is particularly handicapped if he or she is administratively subordinate to positions such as the special collections librarian, radio station manager, or physical plant director. Administrators and key faculty members tend to look at these directors as marginal players "with minor responsibilities, dubious academic credentials, and work which is peripheral to the mainstream of academic priorities" (Wunsch, 1991). It is easy to see why Konomos (1991) found that two of the leading frustrations of media center directors are lack of authority and lack of respect.

Most of the positions in an instructional technology support unit are at the technical level and require minimal educational qualifications. However, the director and key subordinates who serve in a consulting capacity should possess the academic credentials, experience levels, and knowledge of college teaching processes at least commensurate with those of the faculty members and administrators with whom they interact. It is incumbent on administrators to write sensible job descriptions for media director positions, emphasizing those qualifications that will allow the director to establish credibility with faculty, move effectively within the upper circles of the institution, become directly involved in key institutional processes, and compete for funding. Search committees for vacant positions must set high expectations and have the persistence to reopen the search if a suitable candidate is not found.

Conclusion

There is little question that instructional technology will have a profound influence on college and university teaching in the twenty-first century, and that it will have considerable penetration by the year 2001. Yet, campuswide instructional technology service units appear to be at a crossroads in 1992. Hazen (this volume) has described the transitional period facing academic computing centers. Campus media centers, too, are facing close scrutiny by administrators under the pressure of declining financial resources. It is possible that many of these centers will not survive the decade.

A number of campuses appear to be looking at decentralization of media services as a means of cutting operating costs. Approximately 12 percent of all college and university campuses do not have centralized media centers, a figure remarkably consistent across Carnegie classifications. Decentralization reduces costs only by stifling or frustrating faculty attempts to use technology in their teaching, hardly a desirable outcome. Decentralization invariably leads to gross inequities in access from one department to another, inefficient purchasing, lack of equipment compatibility across campus, storerooms full of equipment needing repairs, and the absence of an office to call for assistance. The abandonment of centralized media services also raises the question of responsibility for installation and maintenance of instructional technology equipment in general-use classrooms.

As the only campuswide service agency solely dedicated to support of the instructional mission of the institution, rather than to research or other functions, the media center should take a leadership role in equipping and preparing faculty for twenty-first-century teaching, collaborating with the library, academic computing center, and other campus agencies in the process. Yet, on many campuses, media centers operate under conditions that make this mission virtually impossible. It is imperative that administrators recognize the essential roles that media service organizations play in supporting instruction, place them in reporting relationships that will let them succeed, and ensure that their directors have the credentials and professional skills necessary to give the centers a high level of credibility in the campus environment.

References

Albright, M. J. "It's Time to Rethink Instructional Technology Services in Higher Education." *TechTrends*, 1989, *34* (5), 40–45.

Albright, M. J. "A Profile of the Profession as We Enter the Last Decade of the Century." Paper presented at the annual spring conference of the Consortium of College and University Media Centers, Philadelphia, May 1991.

Association for Educational Communications and Technology. *The Definition of Educational Technology*. Washington, D.C.: Association for Educational Communications and Technology, 1977.

Consortium of College and University Media Centers. *Report of 1991 Information Exchange Committee Survey*. Ames: Consortium of College and University Media Centers Executive Office, Media Resources Center, Iowa State University, 1992.

Gilbert, S. W. "Tomorrow's Faculty and Information Technology: An Opportunity Lost?" *EUIT Newsletter*, 1990, *4* (2), 6.

Konomos, P. "Media Centers: Concerns and Priorities." *Leader*, 1991, *20* (1), 11–12.

Wunsch, M. A. "Killing the Old Myths: Positioning an Instructional Technology Center for a New Era in Higher Education." Paper presented at the fall conference of the Consortium of College and University Media Centers, Honolulu, Hawaii, October 1991.

MICHAEL J. ALBRIGHT is director of the Center for Instructional Support, University of Hawaii at Manoa, Honolulu.

How do faculty development, instructional development, organizational development, and personal development activities contribute to the improvement of instruction?

Faculty Development's Role in Improving Undergraduate Education

David L. Graf, Michael J. Albright, Daniel W. Wheeler

For many years, the focus of instructional quality control in higher education was on subject matter competence. It was assumed that if a professor had mastery of a discipline, he or she would be able to teach it to others. Selectivity in hiring faculty members theoretically led to quality teaching (Sullivan, 1983). By the early 1970s, factors such as a period of retrenchment following two decades of "boom" proportions, decreasing mobility and declining morale among faculty members, an increasingly heterogeneous student body, and rapidly changing subject matter in many disciplines led colleges and universities to reassess the need for faculty training and support services.

This is the environment that spawned the faculty development movement. Officials on many campuses concluded that systematic activities devoted to assisting faculty members could help them deal with some of these emerging areas of concern. Sullivan (1983) reported that only forty to fifty faculty development programs existed at the end of the 1960s, but, by November 1975, 1,044 colleges and universities, or 60 percent of all four-year institutions in the United States, maintained organized faculty development or instructional improvement programs (Centra, 1976). A more recent survey by Erickson (1986) found that nearly half of all baccalaureate institutions still maintained faculty development programs.

Current trends in services known variously as faculty, instructional, organizational, and personal development are described in this chapter. The chapter also addresses the qualifications and activities of faculty development staff, the threats to faculty development programs, and the future of the faculty development movement.

Definitions and Focus of Activities

Services provided by a faculty development center may take different forms, serve different purposes, and be directed toward different groups of participants. While all are intended ultimately to foster instructional improvement, some do so on a long-range basis.

Faculty Development. Faculty development (FD) is a systematic effort to increase effectiveness in all professorial roles, including teaching. According to Nelson (1981, p. 22), FD refers to those activities "designed to improve faculty performance in all aspects of their professional lives—as teachers, scholars, advisors, academic leaders, and contributors to institutional decisions." Gaff (1975, p. 14) defined FD as "enhancing the talents, expanding the interests, improving the competence, and otherwise facilitating the professional and personal growth of faculty members, particularly in their role as instructors."

FD efforts thus are directed primarily toward the teaching and other professional skills of individual faculty members. While FD centers often provide one-on-one consultations with individual faculty members, many activities are open to or intended for the faculty as a whole. Typical programs include seminars and workshops, peer support group meetings, newsletters, mentoring programs, new-faculty orientations, travel grant programs, and resource libraries open to all faculty members.

Instructional Development. Whereas FD activities are focused on the skills and attitudes of the faculty, instructional development (ID) is oriented toward improving the conditions under which learning takes place (Gaff, 1975). Gaff (1975, p. 47) defined ID as "the systematic and continuous application of learning principles and educational technology to develop the most effective and efficient learning experiences for students." ID activities may be concerned with either the processes (methods) used in the learning environment or the products (learning materials) incorporated within that environment. Typical tasks include basic course design or revision, preparation of learning activities for students, and development or adaptation of learning materials, such as videotapes, workbooks, or computer software. ID in this form is almost always conducted with individual faculty members or teams working on specific projects.

The differentiation between ID and FD is somewhat clouded when it comes to helping faculty improve their teaching skills. Although Gaff believed that this activity was clearly FD, Bergquist and Phillips (1975), Lindquist (1978), Albright (1988), and others felt that all activities related to the improvement of an instructor's performance in the classroom were ID functions. The semantics are unimportant, as long as the support services are provided. ID in this form involves most of the program types described above in the FD description. In-depth learning activities (from two to fourteen days in length) and organizational assessments related to improving the campus environment for teaching have also emerged.

Organizational Development. Organizational development (OD) attempts to bring about instructional improvement by changing the environment in which the faculty member operates (Gaff, 1975). OD activities often feature strategies that encourage institutional renewal and increased organizational effectiveness. Organizational developers typically are involved in activities such as conducting training in management and interpersonal relations for department chairs and other campus leaders, improving intracampus communications, resolving issues related to instructional facilities, conducting participative problem-solving sessions, and assisting the institution and its individual components in goal-setting activities and strategic planning. Types of OD methods include workshops and retreats, open forums, committee and task force work, and meetings with individuals or small groups.

Personal Development. Personal development (PD) takes a more holistic approach to the individual faculty member by attempting to enhance interpersonal skills, promote wellness, and assist with career planning. According to Lindquist (1978, p. 57), PD helps faculty members to "reduce personal obstacles to teaching effectiveness and strengthen opportunities for personal and professional advancements related to teaching."

PD activities often focus on strategies and experiences that explore and develop intra- and interpersonal effectiveness. Included are career planning programs and development of assertiveness and personal attending skills. PD formats typically involve individual consultations, workshops and seminars, peer support group meetings, and retreats.

Emerging Activities and Trends

Although during the early 1980s a few highly visible FD centers were closed, each year a number of new centers are established. This trend has been reflected in attendance rates at the preconference New Faculty Developers Workshop conducted by the Professional and Organizational Development (POD) Network in Higher Education. The POD Network, the primary professional organization for developers, has grown virtually every year since its establishment in 1976 to a present membership of nearly seven hundred, including faculty, professional faculty developers, administrators, students, and professional consultants.

With the many calls (National Commission on Excellence in Education, 1983; National Institute of Education, 1984) for reform and change in postsecondary education, FD centers will undoubtedly be asked to play major roles in helping faculty and institutions address these issues. Many colleges and universities are expanding the scope of activities under the

FD umbrella with the understanding that FD is closely tied to institutional vitality (Splete, Austin, and Rice, 1990; Clark and Lewis, 1985; Baldwin, 1985). The following are emerging priorities:

Establishment and Retention of New Faculty. Many institutions provide extensive and intensive activities to orient and support new faculty (Creswell and others, 1990). Formal orientations on an institutionwide basis are often supplemented by formal or informal orientations offered at the college or department level. Mentoring programs for junior faculty members are also available at a number of institutions. Long Beach State University in California and the University of Georgia have exemplary mentoring programs. Peer visit programs have also begun to emerge, with a major study on this topic just completed at the University of Maryland. Mentoring and peer visit programs can be particularly valuable in retaining female and minority faculty members entering college teaching, but all new faculty can benefit from these opportunities.

Multicultural Sensitivity. Minority enrollment in the nation's colleges and universities increased 33 percent between 1976 and 1986, and ethnic minorities constituted 17 percent of all incoming, full-time college freshmen by 1988 (Carter, 1990). The task of helping faculty understand the characteristics, value systems, and learning styles of a rapidly changing student body has become an important function of FD programs. The University of Hawaii at Manoa and the University of Missouri at Columbia are examples of institutions with well-focused programs in this area.

Leadership and Support of Department Chairs. Department chairs are essentially front-line faculty developers (Creswell and others, 1990; Tucker, 1984). Workshops, seminars, and individual consultation to chairs on the facilitation of faculty growth have become increasingly important functions of FD programs, along with other activities under the rubric of OD. Well-developed department chair support programs exist at the University of Nebraska at Lincoln and Fairleigh Dickinson University.

Preparation of Teaching Assistants. Teaching assistants (TAs) are an essential component of the faculty at most universities and carry much of the teaching load in lower-division courses. Many institutions have established active programs for training TAs in such areas as course organization and management, basic teaching methods, and campus resources. Activities often include microteaching, classroom observations, and videotaping. Issues related to international TAs have received special attention. The Universities of Washington, Texas at Austin, Nebraska, Michigan, and Colorado, Syracuse University, and Ohio State University, among others, have developed extensive TA training programs, and a national conference is now held annually on the topic. These programs play a vital role in the preparation of the professoriate of the future and can make an important difference in the quality of undergraduate education today.

Assessment. Campus leaders are being held increasingly accountable by regents and legislatures for the quality of education provided at their institutions. Quality of instructional programs is often measured in this context by the skills and knowledge of graduates at commencement or after their entry into the labor force. Faculty developers are sometimes called on to help their institutions design assessment measures to meet these requirements. The University of Tennessee is recognized as a leader in the assessment field. Since serious issues can be raised regarding how student assessment results are used, faculty developers need to be careful in defining their roles so that consulting relationships with faculty are not compromised.

Holistic or Enhanced Faculty Development. Schuster, Wheeler, and Associates (1990) note that a number of institutions are moving to more systematic, comprehensive FD programs that place greater emphasis on PD and OD. A prime example is the University of Georgia, which incorporates a wide range of professional and personal activities.

Distance Education. At many institutions, distance education technology has become increasingly important in the delivery of credit courses, workshops, and other continuing education activities. The distance education environment is quite different from that of the standard classroom. Comprehensive training programs are required to help inexperienced faculty operate effectively in the distance education environment. FD specialists are now being asked to provide these services in support of distance education activities. The University of Wisconsin and Virginia Tech are among the institutions that have established active training programs for faculty involved in teaching at a distance.

Preparation of Part-Time Faculty. Most colleges and universities have used part-time faculty for years; but as economic pressures mount, use of part-time personnel is likely to increase. Many of these individuals have had limited higher education experience and no training in course management and instructional methods. FD programs can provide essential support services in these areas. A good source of strategies is the program in place at California State University at Fullerton.

Curriculum Development. A number of academic deans use curriculum development as a means to achieve FD. Certainly, FD and ID can enhance consultation on course and curriculum design or redesign. A longstanding leader is the Syracuse University Center for Instructional Development.

Staffing of Faculty Development Programs

FD programs are typically staffed in one of three ways: a full-time staff member hired specifically for the position, experienced faculty members in academic departments serving part-time as FD specialists, or graduate students fulfilling assistantships in the center. Some larger centers have more than one full-time individual and may also have part-time faculty consultants and graduate assistants.

Sell and Chism (1991) have described the advantages and disadvantages of each of these arrangements. Full-time professionals were the option of choice for institutions that can afford them, although each of the other two alternatives has its merits. Advantages brought to FD programs by full-time specialists can include greater stability and continuity; full-time commitment to the functions of the position, rather than teaching, research obligations, or graduate study; professional training and experience as a faculty developer; and greater commitment to professional activity and personal growth in the FD field. Existing faculty serving as part-time faculty developers are more likely to have established respect and status within the institution and to have more experience in college teaching. Moreover, professors from a variety of academic departments, serving as part-time developers, may be better able to accommodate faculty needs from a broad spectrum of disciplines. This option also seems to have the greatest cost savings.

The FD programs at many smaller institutions are managed by faculty committees, with members serving on a rotating basis. A recent survey by Lunde and Healy (1991) found that these committees are generally successful in providing workshops, publications and other educational materials, and grants for faculty travel or other instructional improvement activities. The meeting time commitment for FD committees averaged less than two hours per month.

What are the typical professional skills required of a faculty developer? Sell and Chism (1991, pp. 23-24) identified seven generic competencies of primary importance: "(1) engage in needs assessment activities; (2) design and develop strategies that promote individual, pedagogical, curricular, and organizational growth; (3) organize and implement specific programs, projects, and studies; (4) plan and deliver oral presentations; (5) conduct research about teaching and learning, and the evaluation of instruction; (6) produce print and non-print communications; and (7) establish and maintain consulting relationships."

Appropriate academic preparation for professional faculty developers is an issue currently receiving much attention in the field. ID has been an academic field of study since the late 1960s, with more than a dozen institutions offering master's and doctoral programs. However, these programs primarily concentrate on curriculum development at the K-12 level, the preparation of training and development personnel for business and government settings, and computer-based product development. Although some institutions, such as Syracuse University and Indiana University, provide graduate assistants with practical experience working with faculty clients, little attention is generally given to the unique nature of ID at the higher education level.

Although many colleges and universities offer courses in college teaching, no institution has ever developed a graduate program specifically for the purpose of preparing faculty developers for higher education settings. Some individuals have been able to tailor their own FD majors through interdisciplinary and independent study courses. Others come to the field with degrees in related fields, such as educational psychology or higher education administration. Most practicing faculty developers today have attained their skills through self-study, attendance at conferences and workshops, networking, and on-the-job experience.

Fortunately, opportunities for professional development in this field are many. In addition to the POD Network's annual conference and Institute for Faculty Developers, many national and international conferences and workshops are held on topics related to college teaching each year. Most are prominently advertised in the *Chronicle of Higher Education* and other publications. The POD Network recently inaugurated a computer-based electronic message service for its members.

Threats to Faculty Development Programs

As with all other support services, FD programs in these hard economic times are being scrutinized for possible cost-saving opportunities. Other factors, too, can influence the degree of success enjoyed by FD centers, including their responsiveness to faculty needs, the relative importance of teaching in the campus system, the stigmatization of clients of these programs as faculty members whose teaching is substandard, and the vested interests of professors who feel that funding for instructional improvement programs is better spent to support research, salaries, or professional travel (Lindquist, 1978). Hammons and Wallace (1976) identified sixteen other factors that jeopardize FD programs. Among them are the failures to assign administrative responsibility for FD, involve faculty in planning and program development, reward participation, provide adequate publicity, and evaluate the results.

Future of Faculty Development

As with other campus programs and services, FD must survive the economic crises currently facing higher education. However, the need for FD programs is stronger now than it has ever been before. All indications point to an extraordinary turnover among faculty during the upcoming decade, bringing large numbers of inexperienced teachers into our classrooms. New technologies promise to transform basic college teaching processes. Both the student body and the faculty will become more ethnically diverse, increasing the need for cultural sensitivity. The curricula in many disciplines must be retuned to meet the rapidly changing needs of the marketplace. Institutions with active, responsive, well-supported FD programs will be well-positioned for success in this period of transition.

References

Albright, M. J. "Cooperation Among Campus Agencies Involved in Instructional Improvement." In E. C. Wadsworth (ed.), *Professional and Organizational Development in Higher Education: A Handbook for New Practitioners.* Stillwater, Okla.: New Forums Press, 1988.

Baldwin, R. *Incentives for Faculty Vitality.* New Directions for Higher Education, no. 51. San Francisco: Jossey-Bass, 1985.

Bergquist, W. H., and Phillips, S. R. *Handbook for Faculty Development.* Vol. 1. Washington, D.C.: Council for the Advancement of Small Colleges, 1975.

Carter, D. J. *Racial and Ethnic Trends in College Participation: 1976 to 1988.* Research Briefs, vol. 1, no. 3. Washington, D.C.: Division of Policy Analysis and Research, American Council on Education, 1990.

Centra, J. *Faculty Development Practices in the United States.* Princeton, N.J.: Educational Testing Service, 1976.

Clark, S. M., and Lewis, D. R. *Faculty Vitality and Institutional Productivity: Critical Perspectives for Higher Education.* New York: Teachers College Press, 1985.

Creswell, J., and others. *Academic Chairperson's Handbook.* Lincoln: University of Nebraska Press, 1990.

Erickson, G. "A Survey of Faculty Development Practices." *To Improve the Academy,* 1986, 5, 182–196.

Gaff, J. G. *Toward Faculty Renewal: Advances in Faculty, Instructional, and Organizational Development.* San Francisco: Jossey-Bass, 1975.

Hammons, J. O., and Wallace, T.H.S. "Sixteen Ways to Kill a College Faculty Development Program." *Educational Technology,* 1976, 16 (12), 16–20.

Lindquist, J. "Approaches to Collegiate Teaching Improvement." In J. Lindquist (ed.), *Designing Teaching Improvement Programs.* Berkeley, Calif.: Pacific Soundings Press, 1978.

Lunde, J. P., and Healy, M. M. *Doing Faculty Development by Committee.* Stillwater, Okla.: New Forums Press, 1991.

National Commission on Excellence in Education. *A Nation at Risk: The Imperative for Educational Reform.* Washington, D.C.: National Commission on Excellence in Education, 1983.

National Institute of Education. *Involvement in Learning: Realizing the Potential of American Higher Education.* Final Report of the Study Group on the Condition of Excellence in American Higher Education. Washington, D.C.: National Institute of Education, 1984.

Nelson, W. *Renewal of the Teacher Scholar.* Washington, D.C.: Association of American Colleges, 1981.

Schuster, J. H., Wheeler, D. W., and Associates. *Enhancing Faculty Careers: Strategies for Development and Renewal.* San Francisco: Jossey-Bass, 1990.

Sell, G. R., and Chism, N. V. "Finding the Right Match: Staffing Faculty Development Centers." *To Improve the Academy,* 1991, 10, 19–29.

Splete, A., Austin, A., and Rice, E. (eds.). *Community Commitment and Congruence: A Different Kind of Excellence.* Washington, D.C.: Council of Independent Colleges, 1990.

Sullivan, L. L. "Faculty Development: A Movement on the Brink." *College Board Review,* 1983, 127, 20–21, 29–31.

Tucker, A. *Chairing the Academic Department: Leadership Among Peers.* (2nd ed.) New York: American Council on Education and Macmillan, 1984.

DAVID L. GRAF *is coordinator for instructional development at the Media Resources Center, Iowa State University, Ames.*

MICHAEL J. ALBRIGHT *is director, Center for Instructional Support, University of Hawaii at Manoa, Honolulu.*

DANIEL W. WHEELER *is director, Office of Professional and Organizational Development, University of Nebraska, Lincoln.*

INDEX

AAHE. *See* American Association for Higher Education

Academic computing, 43–45; future strategies for, 50–52; and impact on the teaching-learning process, 46–48; obstacles in, 49–50; trends in, 48–49. *See also* Microcomputers

Adrianson, L., 58–59

Africa, 56, 61–62

Agency for Educational Development, 1

Albright, M. J., 11–12, 92, 96–98, 102

American Association for the Advancement of Science, 87

American Association for Higher Education (AAHE), 96

American Journal of Distance Education, 71

American Library Association, 89–90

Ames Research Center (NASA), 80

Analytical graphics, 17

Anderson, J. A., 2

Apple Company, 31n, 41, 44

Arias, A., 58–59

Arizona, University of, 57

Artificial Reality, 80

Artificial reality. *See* Virtual reality

Asia, 61

Association for Computer Machinery's Special Interest Group-Graphics, 80

Association for Educational Communications and Technology, 9, 92

Association of Research Libraries, 87

AT&T, 68

Audio, 35; in computer conferencing, 60, 62n; in distance education, 70–71; in multimedia systems, 33–35; in virtual reality, 79

Austin, A., 103–104

Baldwin, R., 103–104

Barron, A., 34–35

Bationo, B. D., 36

Bellman, B., 58–59

Bergquist, W. H., 102

Binational English and Spanish Telecommunications Network (BESTNET), 57–58; access to new learning environments in, 60; evaluating student

outcomes in, 58–60; globalizing, 61–62; research findings for, 60–61

Boeing, 80

Borzo, J., 30

Boyer, E. L., 49–50

Brand, S., 66

Bricken, M., 78, 80–81

Bridging the Distance, 69

Briggs, L. J., 11

Brigham Young University, 2

Britain, 56

British Open University, 57, 66–67

Brooks, F., 80

Bulletin boards. *See* Computer electronic messaging

Burns, K., 38

Business departments, 37–38, 47

Business Week, 71

Bylinsky, G., 79

Caldwell, R., 57

California State University System, 2, 61–62, 105

Canada, 56–57, 61

Carl, D. R., 73

Carlson, P. A., 36

Carnegie Commission on Higher Education, 1

Carnegie Foundation classifications, 96–97, 99

Carter, D. J., 104

CAUSE, 87

CD-ROM (compact disk-read only memory), 35, 38, 85–86

Centra, J., 101

Channel One, 13

Charles, J., 66

Child, W. C., Jr., 45

Chism, N. V., 106

Chronicle of Higher Education, 2, 98, 107

Cichocki, R. R., 2

Clark, R. E., 24

Clark, S. M., 103–104

Clark, T. A., 65

Classrooms, multimedia, 33, 38–39, 50

Closed-circuit television systems (CCTV), 91

Coalition for Networked Information (CNI), 87
College and University Systems Exchange (CAUSE), 87
Colorado College, 56
Colorado, University of, 104
Communication, 19; computer electronic messaging as, 55-62; in learning environments, 33, 36
Compact Disk-Interactive (CD-I) systems, 41
Compressed Air, 80
Computer conferencing, 55; in distance education, 66, 72, 75; history of, 56-57; as virtual classrooms, 56-58, 62n. See also Computer electronic messaging
Computer electronic messaging, 54-55; BESTNET experiment in, 57-62; and history of conferencing, 56-57
Computer Graphics, 80
Computer Graphics Metafile, 22
Computers. See Microcomputers
Conceptualization, 19-21
Conferencing. See Computer conferencing
Consortium of College and University Media Centers, 96
Conway, K. L., 2, 39, 45
Cornell University, 36
Corporations. See Industry
Correspondence study. See Distance education
Costs, 18; for distance education, 74; of media centers, 99; of microcomputers, 44, 50; of multimedia, 37, 50; of presentation graphics, 23, 26; of virtual reality, 79. See also Funding
Courteau, J., 87
Crane, G., 38
Creation, 19-21
Creswell, J., 104
Cuban, L., 49-50
Cyberspace. See Virtual reality

Davenport, G., 37-38
Davis, L. M., 21
Dede, C., 45
Delaware, University of, 40
Desktop systems: for multimedia, 41; for publishing, 52; video for, 29-30, 48
Diamond, R. M., 8
Dickens, J. L., 2
Dickie, K. E., 24

Digital storage media, 35, 41
Distance education, 29, 65, 91; conferencing for, 55-56, 58-59; criteria for successful systems of, 68-69; electronic networking for, 48-49; faculty development for, 105; future of, 74-75; higher education's role in, 67-68; implications for teachers of, 71-74; media centers as support for, 95; trends in, 69-71; universities founded for, 66-67. See also Binational English and Spanish Telecommunications Network
Distribution, 19-21
Dolence, M. G., 45
Dougherty, R. M., 83
Douglas, J. V., 45
Duggan, B., 2
Dwyer, F. M., 24

Earnest, C., 3
Edison, T., 49
Educational Uses of Information Technology (EUIT), 96
EDUCOM (Interuniversity Communications Council), 87, 96
Electronic displays, 28
Electronic images, 26
Electronic Information Exchange System, 56-57
Electronic mail, 55, 75. See also Computer electronic messaging
Electronic networking, 48-49
Electronic photography, 29
Electronic studio, 20-22
Elmore, G. C., 2, 39-40
Erickson, G., 101
Europe: computer conferencing in, 56-59, 61, 62n

Faculty development, 101; activities for, 102-105; for distance education, 69, 73-74; future of, 107-108; and integration of multimedia, 39-40; media centers for, 91, 95; programs for, 105-107; support services for, 11-12, 73, 95; trends for, 103-105. See also Faculty members
Faculty members, 86, 89, 101; benefits of computers for, 46; distance education and implications for, 71-74; electronic studios for, 20-22; graphics use by, 18-23, 28, 30-31n; guidelines on

presentation materials for, 26-27; as instructional technologists, 8-10; need for support services by, 11-12, 73; resistance to use of technology by, 1-2, 7, 9, 12, 14, 49; technology literacy of, 10-12, 49-50; and technology use in the future, 13-14. *See also* Faculty development

Fairleigh Dickinson University, 104
Fawson, E. C., 2, 38-40
Feenberg, A., 56
Fontana, L. A., 38
Fraley, L. E., 9-10
France, 56
Fridlund, A. J., 27
Friedlander, L., 38
Fritz, M., 80-81
Frye, T. W., 73
Fund for the Improvement of Post-Secondary Education, 60
Funding, 7, 29, 45; for academic computing, 50-51; for distance education, 74-75; for faculty development, 74; for integration of multimedia, 40; for media centers, 97; for presentation graphics, 23; for technology by industry vs. by education, 13-14. *See also* Costs; Support services

Gaff, J. G., 1, 102-103
Gagne, R. M., 11
Gay, G. K., 36
Gehlauf, D. N., 73
General Motors, 68
George Mason University, 38
Georgia, University of, 104-105
Germany, 56
Gilbert, S. W., 2, 96
Graphics, 52; in distance education, 70-71; in media centers, 94-95; in virtual reality, 78. *See also* Presentation graphics
Green, D., 27
Green, K. C., 7
Griffin, S., 39
Grimes, J., 79
Guelph, University of, 57

Halstead, K., 84
Hammons, J. O., 107
Harasim, L., 57
Harber, J. D., 37-38

Hardware, 18; for desktop video, 29-30; in distance education, 74; IBM computers, 34, 44; Macintosh computers, 31n, 34, 44; mainframe computers, 43-44; for multimedia, 30; for presentation graphics, 28, 30-31n
Hart, M. S., 87
Harvard University, 38
Hawaii, University of, 104
Hazen, M., 45, 99
Head, J. T., 19, 23, 26
Healy, M. M., 106
Hezel, R. T., 70, 75
High-Performance Computing Act, 87
Hiltz, S. R., 56-59, 62n
Hjelmquist, E., 58-59
Holmberg, B., 72
Holography, 41, 66
Honeywell, 68
Human Interface Technology Laboratory, 80
Humanities departments: computer applications for, 38, 47; computer conferencing for, 57-62
Hunter, B., 49
Hypermedia environments, 35-37, 66

IBM Corporation, 34, 41, 44, 68, 74-75
IEEE Computer Graphics and Applications, 80
Illinois, University of, 36, 44
Image classification model, 23-24, 30n
Indiana University, 106
Indiana University-Purdue University, 2, 38-40
Industry: computer conferencing in, 62n; distance education and needs of, 69-70; funds for technology by, 13; presentation graphics systems in, 18; teamwork and collaboration skills in, 36
Instructional development, 8-9
Instructional technology: and academic computing, 43-52; computer electronic messaging in, 55-62; in distance education, 65-75; explanation of, 8-10, 92; faculty development for, 101-108; and faculty members, 7-14; in media centers, 91-99; multimedia as, 33-41; potential of, 1-3; presentation graphics as, 17-31; and research libraries, 83-90; and virtual reality, 77-81

Integrated Instructional Technology Services model, 92–93
International Council on Correspondence Education, 71–72
Interuniversity Communications Council (EDUCOM), 87, 96
Iowa State University, 12
Iowa, University of, 40

Japan, 56
Johnson, J., 47
Jones, L. J., 36

Kastner, C., 49
Kaye, T., 57–59
Kearsley, G., 75
Keegan, D., 65, 72
Kelly, M., 65
Kent State University, 2
Kerr, E., 56–59
Kerstetter, J. P., 2
Knapper, C. K., 7, 10
Knowlton, J. Q., 23
Konomos, P., 96, 98
Kozma, R. B., 47, 49
Krueger, M., 80

Lamb, A., 36
Languages, foreign: computer applications for, 47–48; computer conferencing for, 57–62, 68
Lanier, J., 80
Lassner, D., 97
Latin America, 56, 61–62
Law schools: computer applications for, 47–48
Leach, R., 57
Leadership: in faculty development, 104; in media centers, 97–99
Learning at the Back, 71
Leiblum, M., 44
Levie, W. H., 24
Levinson, P., 57
Lewis, D. R., 103–104
Lewis, R. J., 7, 10
Libraries, 51, 83; alternatives to print in, 84–86; automation of, 44–45; in distance education, 73; of the future, 86–88; and information literacy, 89–90; and media centers, 96–97; roles of librarians and users in, 88–89; support services for, 11–12

Lindquist, J., 102–103, 107
Liquid crystal display (LCD) panels, 35
Lockwood, A. F., 19
Long Beach State University, 104
Lunde, J. P., 106
Lyman, P., 84
Lynch, C. A., 86

McEwen, J. W., 36
McGraw-Hill, 2
MacGregor, A. J., 18, 26
McNeil, D. R., 1, 7
Maine, Community College of, 67
Maine, University of, 67
Marek, S., 2
Maricopa Community College, 57
Maryland, University of, 104
Massachusetts Institute of Technology, 37, 66
Mathematics departments: computer applications for, 37, 58
Media centers, 8, 86, 91–92; barriers to success of, 95–99; decentralization of, 99; high–resolution output services in, 28; for integration of multimedia, 40; roles of, 1, 93–95; support services for, 11–12
Media formats, 24–26, 66; in distance education, 72; in media centers, 93–94; for multimedia, 33. *See also individual media*
Medical schools: computer applications for, 47
Mexico, 60
Michigan, University of, 104
Microcomputers: background of, in education, 44, 91; on campuses, 3, 11, 39, 45; in distance education, 66, 73; impact of, on teaching and learning, 7, 46–48; in multimedia systems, 34, 41; for presentation graphics, 30. *See also Academic computing*
Microforms, 85
Mid-America, University of, 1, 66–67
Miller, R. L., 37
Minno, R. A., 2
Missouri, University of, 104
Mitre Corporation, 44
Modems, 66
Mohl, B., 41
Monson, M. K., 69
Moore, D. M., 26

Moore, M., 72
Multimedia, 13, 72; applications for, 37–38; in classrooms, 33, 38–39, 50; components of, 34–35; future of, 41; integration of, in teaching-learning process, 39–40; as interactive learning environments, 33, 35–37; in media centers, 94; for presentation graphics, 29–30
Multisensory interactive interface devices, 78
Myers, D., 36

Nairobi, University of, 61–62
NASA, 80
Nash, J. M., 23
Nasser, L. D., 36
National Commission on Excellence in Education, 103
National Institute of Education, 103
National Research and Education Network (NREN), 49, 87
National Science Foundation, 61–62
National Technological University, 2, 70
Naval Postgraduate School, 80
Nebraska, University of, 104
Nelson, W., 102
Networking, 45, 48–49
Networks, 34, 44–45; Binational English and Spanish Telecommunications Network, 57–62; for distance education, 56, 68; for faculty development, 103, 107; for hypermedia environments, 36; as key central services, 50–51; for multimedia, 40; for national and international libraries, 87; trends in, 48–49
New Faculty Developers Workshop, 103
New Jersey Institute of Technology (NJIT), 56
New School for Social Research, 57
New Science and Mechanical Engineering, 80
'New Video Network at Texas A&M University System', 2
New York Institute of Technology, 57
New York, State University of, 2
Nicol, A., 36
NJIT. See New Jersey Institute of Technology
Noblitt, J. S., 39
Norgaard, C., 37
North Carolina, University of: multime-dia projects at, 2, 39; virtual reality at, 77–78, 80
Northwestern University, 77–78

Ohio State University, 104
Oklahoma State University, 13
Online Computer Library Center (OCLC), 87
Online public access catalogs (OPACs), 84
Ontario Institute for Studies in Education, 57
Overhead projectors: for multimedia presentations, 35; transparencies for presentations, 25–26, 28

Pea, R. D., 36
Pennsylvania State University, 40
Penrod, J. I., 45
Periodical index system, 84–85
Peters, P. E., 87
Pfaffenberger, B., 17
Phillips, S. R., 102
POD Network, 103, 107
Polley, E., 1
Presentation graphics, 17–18, 52; and developing technologies, 29–30; and electronic studios, 20–22; guidelines for materials for, 26–27; implications of, for teaching and learning, 22–24; media formats for, 24–26; models in the presentation process, 19–21; system components for, 28, 30–31n; trends in, 29
President's Commission on Instructional Technology, 8
Private industry. See Industry
Production, 19–21
Professional and Organizational Development (POD) Network, 103, 107
Psychology departments: computer applications for, 47
Puttre, M., 78

Ra, M., 88–89
Rabb, M. Y., 26
Randall, J. P., 80–81
Regenstein, C., 45
Research, 51; computer applications for, 46–47; as favored over instructional improvement, 49–50; presentation graphics for, 23, 29. See also Libraries

Rubin, M., 49
Russia, 56

San Diego State University, 57, 59
Sanders, W. H., 23
Scanners, 31n, 35
Schmid, C. F., 22-23
Schmid, S. E., 22-23
Schuster, J. H., 105
Schwebach, L., 3
Science: computer applications for, 37, 47; computer conferencing for, 58, 61
Seidel, R. J., 49
Sell, G. R., 106
Sexism, 59
Shatz, M. A., 73
Slides, 35mm, 25-26, 28
Smith, P., 65, 71
Smith, S. G., 36
Society, 21, 36; pressures by, for technology use in education, 13-14; social change and technology in, 49-52
Software, 7, 11, 18, 46; for computer conferencing, 55; for desktop video, 29-30; development of, 44-45, 51-52; in distance education, 66, 68; for foreign language learning, 47-48; Hyper-Card, 34; hypermedia, 66; IBM Link-way, 34; for multimedia, 72; for presentation graphics, 27-29, 30n; Windows, 30n, 34
Southern California, University of, 2, 45
Splete, A., 103-104
Standard Generalized Markup Language, 22
Stanford University, 38, 77-78
Strang, H. R., 36
Students, 23, 101; in distance education, 68-70, 72; early computer use by, 44, 46; as library users, 86, 89-90; minorities as, 59-60, 104; multimedia projects for, 37-38; nontraditional, 29, 60-61, 68; technological literacy by, 13-14, 49-50
Sullivan, L. L., 101
Support services, 40, 45; decentralization of, 50-51; for distance education, 69, 73; need for, 11-12, 14. See also Funding; Media centers
Sweden, 56
Syracuse University, 104-106
Systems approach, 8

Teaching-learning process: future changes in, 29; impact of computers on, 46-48; implications of presentation graphics for, 22-24; in Information Age, 8-9; multimedia in, 39-40
Technology, 7, 36, 41; capital investment in, by industry vs. by education, 13-14; data glove technology, 78-79; effective use of, 10-11; nonlinear access to information through, 35. See also Instructional technology
Telecommunications, 44-45, 67, 74
Tennessee, University of, 105
Tennyson, R. D., 36
Texas A&M University System, 2
Texas Interactive Instructional Network (TI-IN), 13
Texas, University of, 104
35mm slides. See Slides, 35mm
Thomas, R. J., 36
Tickton, S. G., 8
TI-IN, 13
Tucker, A., 104
Tufte, E. R., 17
Turner Educational Services, 13
Turoff, M., 56-59
Tynan, A., 57

United States: computer conferencing in, 56-57, 60, 62; Department of Defense, 62n
United States Distance Learning Association, 70
United States Office of Technology Assessment, 73
'University of the Future Planned for California', 2
Utilization, 19-21

Van Nest, W., 57
Vanderbilt University, 2
VanUitert, D. D., 2, 38-40
Vargas, E. A., 9-10
Verduin, J. R., Jr., 65
Video, 11, 13; computer conferencing and use of, 58, 60, 62n, 68; in desktop systems, 29-30, 48; in distance education, 70-71, 75; in media centers, 94; in multimedia systems, 33-34; for presentation graphics, 29-30; trends for, 48-49
Virginia Tech, 105

Virtual Classrooms, 56–58, 62n
Virtual library, 86–88
Virtual reality, 66, 77; defined, 78; research and development in, 79–81
Virtual Reality Report and Multimedia Review, 80
Vozick, T., 57
VPL Research, 79–80

Wager, W. W., 11
Wall, M., 7, 10
Wall Street Journal, 71
Wallace, T.H.S., 107
Washington, University of, 77–78, 80, 104

Watkins, B. T., 2, 45
Wedemeyer, C. A., 71
Western Behavioral Sciences Institute, 56, 59
Wheeler, D. W., 105
Wileman, R. E., 22–23
Wilson, D. L., 45
Winn, B., 23
Wisconsin, University of, 67–69, 71, 105
Women, 59–60
Wunsch, M. A., 98

Zigerell, J., 67–68
Zimbabwe, University of, 61–62
Zimmerer, J., 57

OTHER TITLES AVAILABLE IN THE
NEW DIRECTIONS FOR TEACHING AND LEARNING SERIES
Robert J. Menges, Editor-in-Chief
Marilla D. Svinicki, Associate Editor

TL50 Developing New and Junior Faculty, *Mary Deane Sorcinelli, Ann E. Austin*
TL49 Teaching for Diversity, *Laura L. B. Border, Nancy Van Note Chism*
TL48 Effective Practices for Improving Teaching, *Michael Theall, Jennifer Franklin*
TL47 Applying the Seven Principles for Good Practice in Undergraduate Education, *Arthur W. Chickering, Zelda F. Gamson*
TL46 Classroom Research: Early Lessons from Success, *Thomas A. Angelo*
TL45 College Teaching: From Theory to Practice, *Robert J. Menges, Marilla D. Svinicki*
TL44 Excellent Teaching in a Changing Academy: Essays in Honor of Kenneth Eble, *Feroza Jussawalla*
TL43 Student Ratings of Instruction: Issues for Improving Practice, *Michael Theall, Jennifer Franklin*
TL42 The Changing Face of College Teaching, *Marilla D. Svinicki*
TL41 Learning Communities: Creating Connections Among Students, Faculty, and Disciplines, *Faith Gabelnick, Jean MacGregor, Roberta S. Matthews, Barbara Leigh Smith*
TL40 Integrating Liberal Learning and Professional Education, *Robert A. Armour, Barbara S. Fuhrmann*
TL39 Teaching Assistant Training in the 1990s, *Jody D. Nyquist, Robert D. Abbott*
TL38 Promoting Inquiry in Undergraduate Learning, *Frederick Stirton Weaver*
TL37 The Department Chairperson's Role in Enhancing College Teaching, *Ann F. Lucas*
TL36 Strengthening Programs for Writing Across the Curriculum, *Susan H. McLeod*
TL35 Knowing and Doing: Learning Through Experience, *Pat Hutchings, Allen Wutzdorff*
TL34 Assessing Students' Learning, *Robert E. Young, Kenneth E. Eble*
TL33 College Teaching and Learning: Preparing for New Commitments, *Robert E. Young, Kenneth E. Eble*
TL32 Teaching Large Classes Well, *Maryellen Gleason Weimer*
TL31 Techniques for Evaluating and Improving Instruction, *Lawrence M. Aleamoni*
TL30 Developing Critical Thinking and Problem-Solving Abilities, *James E. Stice*
TL29 Coping with Faculty Stress, *Peter Seldin*
TL28 Distinguished Teachers on Effective Teaching, *Peter G. Beidler*
TL27 Improving Teacher Education, *Eva C. Galambos*
TL26 Communicating in College Classrooms, *Jean M. Civikly*
TL25 Fostering Academic Excellence Through Honors Programs, *Paul G. Friedman, Reva Jenkins-Friedman*
TL24 College-School Collaboration: Appraising the Major Approaches, *William T. Daly*
TL23 Using Research to Improve Teaching, *Janet G. Donald, Arthur M. Sullivan*
TL22 Strengthening the Teaching Assistant Faculty, *John D. W. Andrews*
TL21 Teaching as Though Students Mattered, *Joseph Katz*
TL14 Learning in Groups, *Clark Bouton, Russell Y. Garth*
TL12 Teaching Writing in All Disciplines, *C. Williams Griffin*
TL3 Fostering Critical Thinking, *Robert E. Young*
TL2 Learning, Cognition, and College Teaching, *Wilbert J. McKeachie*
TL1 Improving Teaching Styles, *Kenneth E. Eble*

ORDERING INFORMATION

NEW DIRECTIONS FOR TEACHING AND LEARNING is a series of paperback books that presents ideas and techniques for improving college teaching, based both on the practical expertise of seasoned instructors and on the latest research findings of educational and psychological researchers. Books in the series are published quarterly in Fall, Winter, Spring, and Summer and are available for purchase by subscription as well as by single copy.

SUBSCRIPTIONS for 1992 cost $45.00 for individuals (a savings of 20 percent over single-copy prices) and $60.00 for institutions, agencies, and libraries. Please do not send institutional checks for personal subscriptions. Standing orders are accepted.

SINGLE COPIES cost $14.95 when payment accompanies order. (California, New Jersey, New York, and Washington, D.C., residents please include appropriate sales tax.) Billed orders will be charged postage and handling.

DISCOUNTS FOR QUANTITY ORDERS are available. Please write to the address below for information.

ALL ORDERS must include either the name of an individual or an official purchase order number. Please submit your order as follows:
   Subscriptions: specify series and year subscription is to begin
   Single copies: include individual title code (such as TL1)

MAIL ALL ORDERS TO:
   Jossey-Bass Publishers
   350 Sansome Street
   San Francisco, California 94104

FOR SALES OUTSIDE OF THE UNITED STATES CONTACT:
   Maxwell Macmillan International Publishing Group
   866 Third Avenue
   New York, New York 10022